MW00715337

# THE RITE
# OF CONFIRMATION

## Moments When
## Faith Is Strengthened

Peter R. Monkres
and R. Kenneth Ostermiller

*United Church Press*
*Cleveland, Ohio*

United Church Press, Cleveland, Ohio 44115

© 1995 by Peter R. Monkres and R. Kenneth Ostermiller

Biblical quotations are from the New Revised Standard Version of the Bible,
© 1989 by the Division of Christian Education of the National Council of the
Churches of Christ in the U.S.A., and are used by permission

All rights reserved. Published 1995
Printed in the United States of America on acid-free paper

00 99 98 97 96 95   5 4 3 2 1

Library of Congress Cataloging-in-Publication Data
Monkres, Peter R., 1946-
    The rite of confirmation : moments when faith is strengthened /
Peter R. Monkres and R. Kenneth Ostermiller.
        p.   cm.
    Includes bibliographical references and index.
    ISBN 0-8298-1020-X (alk. paper)
    1. Confirmation.   2. Christian education of adults.
I. Ostermiller, R. Kenneth.   II. Title.
BV815.M59   1995
265'.2—dc20                                             94-39954
                                                            CIP

# THE RITE OF CONFIRMATION

# Contents

# Introduction

We want to share with you some radical proposals about the rite of confirmation. It's an exciting time to do this thinking in the life of the church of Jesus Christ. A good deal of spirited discussion surrounds the meaning of the rite of confirmation, and there is a hunger for new resources to make confirmation more meaningful. At the same time, there is a need for more clarity about the role this rite plays in the contemporary church and society. No normative vision currently holds sway. We hope that you, whether pastor or lay person, will use our ideas to reflect on the practice of confirmation in your congregation and consider how you can most faithfully help your church community understand and plan for the rite of confirmation.

The concept of confirmation points to a basic human need all of us seek to have met. The word *confirmation* means to say "yes." As human beings we need to say "yes" and to have a "yes" said to us. We need both to make confirmations and to be confirmed by others. Such affirmations are experiences central to the health of every person. Seen in its broadest and most essential sense, the church's rite of confirmation is connected to the process by which we are personally loved, valued, and respected by others in life, as well as with how we can affirm others.

All people need affirming experiences throughout their lives. Infants need parental love that affirms their worth. Babies who are not affirmed in this way may suffer from delayed development and even death. As they enter the world, children need experiences that affirm their curiosity, creativity, and intelligence. Children not affirmed in this way may lose interest in learning and be unable to fulfill their creative potential. Youth and younger adults need affirmation of their ability to give and receive love. Depression, loneliness, or despair is often the result when intimate relationships are not found. Finally, adults need a community that affirms their worth and supports them as they experience life in parenting, choosing a vocation, entering retirement, and facing death. When the affirming power of such adult communities is absent, one's sense of meaning and significance is diminished.

Such affirmation also plays a critical role in the development of religious life. To mature spiritually, Christians need a place to develop and test their relationship with God, to reflect on the essential theological concepts that are part of the faith tradition, and to enjoy opportunities to serve others. These are the foundation stones of the rite of confirmation. Those who do not have such experiences lack a connection with a confirming community that encourages them to be disciples in the world.

True experiences of confirmation depend on a community of support that helps us know and value ourselves. Because opportunities for community are rare in our society, many people do not experience such moments of confirmation in their lives. In *Habits of the Heart*, Robert Bellah and his colleagues observed:

> There are many truths we do not see when we adopt the language [and experience] of radical individualism. We find ourselves not independently of other people and institutions but through them. We never get to the bottom of ourselves on our own. . . . All of our activity goes on in relationships, groups, associations, and communities ordered by institutional structures and interpreted by cultural patterns of meaning.[1]

The church has endeavored to be a primary community of support for Christians. It has done so by providing compassion, nurture, challenge, and support to all in the name of Christ. Through this practice of love, the church seeks to confirm its members as children of God and encourage them to deepen their faith.

The traditional biblical metaphor for this confirming community is "the body of Christ," in which each person is a "member" who supports and is supported by others. For Paul, the body of Christ is the community in which we confirm one another by bearing one another's burdens and sharing one another's joys (1 Cor. 12:26). Henri Nouwen offers yet another understanding of the body of Christ when he writes in *Reaching Out* that the church confirms persons by offering a supportive space in which each can develop his or her relationship with God:

> *Hospitality . . . means the creation of a free space where the stranger can enter and become a friend instead of an enemy. Hospitality is not to change people, but to offer them space where change can take place. It is not to bring men and women over to our side, but to offer them freedom not disturbed by dividing lines. It is not to lead our neighbor into a corner where there are no alternatives left, but to open a wide spectrum of options for choice and commitment. It is not an educated intimidation with good books, good stories and good works, but the liberation of fearful hearts so that words can find roots and bear ample fruit. It is not a method of making our God and our way into the criteria of happiness, but the opening of an opportunity to others to find their God and their way.[2]*

When the Christian church provides this sort of hospitality, it confirms its members by supporting their journeys of faith and providing a context in which their faith can be examined, tested, and strengthened.

Many in our society long for experiences of true confirmation. The church has a golden opportunity to respond to this yearning by offering ministries that address the major confirming moments in peoples lives. If we could provide such ministries, the rite of confirmation would be revitalized and many lives empowered.

## CHAPTER ONE

# A Rite in Search of Significance

The church's current practice of the rite of confirmation lacks clarity and impact. We usually limit our understanding of this rite to a one- or two-year educational program for junior- and senior-high youth. At the end of this education program, we hope that the young people will choose to become active adult members in the church. This approach to confirmation has failed in both Roman Catholic and Protestant churches. Jesuit theologian Karl Rahner has said of Roman Catholic confirmation: "The sacrament of confirmation does not really play an important part in the life of the average Catholic Christian today."[1]

The problem is equally acute in the mainline or reformation churches. Since the 1950s, a high percentage of the baby boom generation was confirmed into the church in the hope that they would become active adult members. But according to a survey by William McKinney and Wade Clark Roof, 34 percent of this generation has dropped out and stayed out of the churches that confirmed them. A Lilly Foundation study, which consisted of extensive interviews with young adults who were confirmed in the Presbyterian Church (USA) estimated that half of the five hundred adults interviewed did not belong to a community of faith. Still other surveys suggest that as many as 70 percent of the baby boomers have no faith community. For this generation, there has been little bonding with the Christian community. One

1

thirty-four-year-old mother of two young children said: "I look at churches as just upholders of a certain tradition and a certain history, and . . . they generally help people. They bring people together as a community and bear very important traditions for this society. Our society lacks so much, you know. So the churches have great importance. But not for me. [She laughed.] But not for me."

Before seeking a more compelling approach to confirmation, it will be helpful to assess what the church has done in the past. Within the mainline Protestant churches there have been three major approaches to confirmation. The first, often called "confirmation class," is a formal schooling model through which an orderly belief system, scripture, Christian history, and polity are shared with youth. This course of study is most often accomplished through a catechism which prioritizes doctrinal formulation and memorization. A second approach focuses upon the contemporary issues with which youth struggle and the ways the Christian faith can make a difference in their lives. These programs tend to focus on such existential issues as personal identity or the development of personal relationships in the church. The third approach offers programs emphasizing the living out of one's faith. These expressions usually involve an exploration of the "social gospel" and participation in mission projects or work camps. For the most part, these three approaches have not empowered youth to say "yes" to the Christian faith or become active members of the congregations that confirmed them.

As a result, we find ourselves with a central rite of the church that is not fulfilling its stated purpose. Rather than strengthening young people's faith and bonding them to a spirit-filled community, confirmation is graduating them from the church.

There is little doubt that the mainline churches have less influence over people's theology, spirituality, and ethical behavior than in past decades. Many recent books, including Loren Mead's *The Once and Future Church*, have pointed out that:

> The forms and structures, the roles and relationships of the
> churches we have inherited were formed by paradigms that no

*longer work for us. We live in the memory of great ways of under-
standing how to be the church. . . . Those memories surround us
like ruins of an ancient civilization. . . . Our educational institu-
tions and our structures of leadership and service are . . . con-
flicted and at war with themselves.*[2]

In this time of declining influence, it is tempting for us to spend
more time developing survival strategies than seeking new visions that could excite the next generation about Christian faith.
But, preoccupation with the organizational concerns afflicting
the church can keep us from our true ministry and mission. If we
are to initiate new persons into the church, we need visions
capable of inspiring upcoming generations to become Christian.
To discover these visions, we need a more flexible and imagina-
tive theology of confirmation. Rather than portraying it as primarily an educational program or rite of passage for youth, we
need to broaden our perspective by considering that confirmation is a repeatable rite which says "yes" to those moments when
faith is strengthened in the lives of those who have been baptized
into the church.

We believe that claiming a faithful role for confirmation
today is not primarily a matter of producing new "programs" or
"resources" for youth, but of offering a lifelong ministry that
helps Christians to continually recognize ways in which they are
growing in faith. It is particularly tempting to market new youth
programs and resources for confirmation today. Pastors are eager
for curricula that combine sound theology with creative opportunities to involve youth in faith exploration. Parents yearn for
occasions when their children come home from the church ex-
pressing interest in the Bible or asking faith questions. Those who
can respond to such needs will attract instant attention and an enthusiastic following. But, although new programs and resources
are important, the more fundamental need is for the church to
recapture a sound theological understanding of confirmation
that connects the traditions of the ancient church with what it
means to be Christian in the modern world.

## DISCUSSION QUESTIONS

1. Invite those present to remember their own confirmation and to offer a brief description of its impact or lack of impact on their faith. After each person has had an opportunity to share, evaluate the group's experience using the following scale:

| Confirmation had no significant effect on my faith journey. | Confirmation had a modest effect on my faith journey. | Confirmation had a great effect on my faith journey. |
|---|---|---|
| _____ | _____ | |

Discuss the following questions:
- What experience of confirmation is most frequent in your group?
- What factors make confirmation most meaningful to participants?
- What factors keep confirmation from being meaningful?

2. How well is confirmation working in your church at the present time?
- What are its greatest strengths?
- What things most need to be changed?
- What strategies would help your church to change?

## CHAPTER TWO

# A Brief History of Confirmation

## ANCIENT ROOTS AND PRACTICE

The meaning of confirmation has not always been as uncertain as it is today. In the early centuries of the church, confirmation had a clear role within the life of the community of faith. By studying the history of confirmation we can recover some of the power of the rite that has that has been lost in the modern era.

According to Michael Dujarier, confirmation had its greatest meaning in the third century. This was the period when initiation into the Christian church "was carried out with the greatest seriousness and intensity."

Following this "golden age," the role of confirmation in the church steadily declined, and its purpose became more vague. Three distinct periods of confirmation can be identified:

**1–500 C.E.**
The classical period of Christian initiation characterized by unified rites of baptism, confirmation, and eucharist.

**500–1500**
The period of eclipse or decline during which confirmation lost its connection with the rites of Christian initiation and was rationalized as a "second stage" completion of baptism.

## 1500–Present

The period of reformation during which Protestants rejected the sacramental standing of confirmation and replaced it with a program of catechetical instruction which became the prototype for current confirmation programs.[1]

The ancient roots of confirmation have at least four lessons to teach us. The first thing we can learn from our history is that confirmation was powerful in the early church because participants were involved in a vigorous process of spiritual formation. To choose to belong to the church was a weighty decision which often affected one's security and always affected one's lifestyle. Because choosing to become Christian had such serious implications, catechesis, the formal process of instruction that helped one to become a member of the church, was a three-year process.

In our day, we need to recapture the intensity of our ancient roots by offering a faith-forming confirmation that has theological depth, provides a substantive challenge for becoming Christian, and culminates in a potent ritual of initiation that is offered to Christians of all ages. Too many current confirmation programs revolve around the hectic schedules of high-school students. Those entrusted with teaching hope they can offer a few valuable insights to youth, but their efforts are often compromised by football games, debate societies, and after-school jobs. Rather than "binge-feeding" our youth with a single faith-formation program, we need a long-term understanding of confirmation that invites persons and the church community to say "yes" to their faith as it grows through the different stages of life. Of course, some concessions must be made to the realities of modern life. But we want to stress that the church needs to define norms and standards for spiritual literacy and seriously portray the challenge of a life of faith to its members.

The second thing we can learn from our history is that confirmation is a liturgical rite of the church, not primarily an educational program. Confirmation is most powerful when we emphasize its ritual richness. The ancient church offered people confirming moments through the conducting of worship that has been described as the "awe-inspiring rites of Christian initiation." As much as possible, we need to recapture the sense of liturgical mystery and transformation that was part of becoming Christian in the early church.

In the early church, the process of religious instruction culminated in unified rites of baptism, confirmation, and first communion on Easter morning. On the Saturday preceding Easter, those who were to become Christians gathered in one place and spent the night in a prayer vigil. They received from the bishop a laying-on of hands; a formal exorcism, which occurred through a breathing on their faces; and a signing of foreheads, ears, and noses. After this service, candidates for baptism faced to the west and renounced the devil. The liturgical action during this part of the ceremony of initiation varied. Chrysostom (345–407) and Theodore (d. 428) instructed candidates to kneel in adoration and confess their sin. In Syria, by the end of the fifth century, candidates were challenged to "breathe upon the devil," dispelling it with this common gesture of exorcism. There is some evidence that St. Ambrose (337–397) directed prospective members of the church to spit in the devil's face. As the initiation progressed, scripture was read to the candidates, and they were instructed throughout the night by the elders and deacons of the church.

At dawn on Easter Sunday, the Christian community began to pray over the baptismal waters. The earliest formal account of this service is found in the oft-quoted Apostolic Tradition, commonly attributed to Hippolytus (215–220):

> *On the Saturday those who are to receive baptism shall be gathered in one place at the bishop's decision. They shall all be told to pray and to kneel. And he shall lay his hands on them and exorcise all alien spirits, that they may flee out of them and never return into them. And when he has finished exorcising them, he shall breathe into their faces; and when he has signed their foreheads, ears, and noses, he shall raise them up. And they shall spend the whole night in vigil; they shall be read to and instructed. . . . At the time when the cock crows, first let prayer be made over the water.[2]*

7

The first Christians were baptized in natural sources of water rather than formal fonts. Rivers, lakes, ponds, springs, or the ocean were the settings for these early rites of initiation. The prayers which Hippolytus (ca. 170–235) mentions in his early church liturgy were the means by which these natural sources of water were cleansed by the invocation of the Holy Spirit. St. Cyprian (256) observed elsewhere: "The water should first be cleansed and sanctified by the priest, that it may wash away by its baptism the sins of the one who is baptized."

In the early church, baptism was accomplished through immersion. By the end of the first century, the *Didache* gives the following instructions:

> *Concerning baptism, baptize in this way. Having first rehearsed all these things [the liturgy of baptism] baptize in the name of the Father and of the Son and of the Holy Spirit in living water. But if you have not living water, baptize into other water; and if you cannot in cold, in warm. If you have neither, pour water thrice on the head.*[3]

Baptism by immersion gave initiates a unique experience of vulnerability. Candidates for baptism in the early church signaled their willingness to surrender to the Holy Spirit by disrobing and allowing themselves to be baptized unclothed. Early Christian theologians offered different perspectives about this practice:

> *Ambrose with his usual delicacy makes no mention of the stripping in De Sacramentis or De Mysteris, though he does speak of it in another place; the Christian's descent into the Jordan (i.e., the font) recalls [one's] naked entry into life and [one's] naked departure from it, and reminds us to avoid superfluities. Cyril, on the contrary, has no inhibitions against speaking about nakedness: he sees in it an imitation of Christ's nakedness on the cross and a sign that the old [humanity] and the devil have been discarded. He is confident that this is the one occasion when hearers will have experienced no shame in nakedness: in this they resembled Adam's innocence in paradise. M. Righettiti, with less simplicity, reminds us that the sexes were sometimes separated for baptism, that dea-*

8

*conesses in some places attended to the women, that the ancients were used to mixed bathing, and that anyhow baptisteries were discreetly dark.*[4]

The candidates were immersed three times in the water. This immersing was conducted specifically to encourage a mood of awe and to lead Christians to experience a death of the old self and a birth of the new self in Christ. One of the most dramatic accounts of this transforming experience can be found in a sermon given by Cyril of Jerusalem to newly baptized Christians. The address was offered in an ancient church said to be built over the site of Christ's own tomb:

*Then you were conducted by the hand to the holy pool of sacred baptism, just as Christ was conveyed from the cross to the sepulcher close at hand. . . . You made the confession that brings salvation, and submerged yourselves three times in the water and emerged: by this symbolic gesture you were secretly reenacting the burial of Christ three days in the tomb. For just as our Savior spent three days and nights in the hollow bosom of the earth, so you upon first emerging were representing Christ's first day in the earth, and by your immersion his first night. For at night one can no longer see but during the day one has light; so you saw nothing when immersed as if it were night, but you emerged as if to the light of day. In one and the same action, you died and were born; the water of salvation became both tomb and mother for you. What Solomon said of others is apposite to you. On that occasion he said: "There is a time to be born and a time to die" (Eccl. 3:2), but the opposite is true in your case—there is a time to die and a time to be born. A single moment achieves both ends, and your beginning was simultaneous with your death.*

*What a strange and astonishing situation! We did not really die, we were not really buried, we did not really hang from a cross and rise again. Our imitation was symbolic, but our salvation was a reality. Christ truly hung from a cross, was truly buried, and truly rose again. All this he did gratuitously for us, so that we might share his sufferings by imitating them, and gain salvation in actuality. What transcendent kindness! Christ endured nails in*

9

*his hands and feet, and suffered pain; and by letting me partici-*
*pate in the pain without anguish or sweat, he freely bestows salva-*
*tion on me.*[5]

We see, then, that the lengthy preparation for membership in the Christian church and the climactic event of baptism surrounded ancient Christians with poetic metaphors, great drama, and occasionally mystical visions. The ancient rites of initiation were anything but domesticated rituals.

The third thing we can learn from our history is that confirmation found its meaning, not as a separate rite of the church, but in relationship to the sacrament of baptism that it followed and the sacrament of Holy Communion that it preceded. As powerful and dramatic as the ancient rites of baptism, confirmation, and eucharist were, they did not stand on their own. Rather, they acted in concert with one another decisively to initiate new Christians into the church.

The original role of confirmation was to anoint newly baptized Christians with oil, seal their baptism, and invoke God's grace in their lives. As Aidan Kavanagh observes:

> *What the Verona text of AT21 describes at this point is a bishop*
> *performing nothing more or less than a missa, his proper liturgy*
> *for the neophytes. He does this by offering a prayer for them. . . .*
> *They then come under his hand as he anoints them in memory of*
> *their baptismal unction in the name of Jesus the Christ and marks*
> *their foreheads using words that once again invoke the Trinitarian*
> *form of their baptismal confession as they are about to exercise*
> *that confession for the first time in the oblation. This is how their*
> *baptism is publicly sealed, perfected, consummated—not by*
> *adding something to it which it lacked, but by introducing them,*
> *now fully equipped, into its exercise. It is all quite scriptural and*
> *liturgically coherent, even rather elegant.*[6]

Cyril of Jerusalem (315–386) suggested that confirmation was a post-baptismal chrismation that offered to each new Christian "the unction, the emblem of that wherewith Christ was anointed;

and this is the Holy Spirit." Ambrose spoke of confirmation as the offering of a "spiritual seal."

The Greek word used by the early Christians for the seal was *sphragis*. The apostle Paul said: "I bear on my body the mark (*sphragis*) of Jesus" (Gal. 6:18). Additional images from the Hellenistic world enriched the church's understanding of this concept. In the agricultural society of Greece, a *sphragis* was a sheep brand. The word was also used to refer to the mark of army enlistment, and it signified the tattoo of a slave. Christ's seal, as offered through confirmation, was the indelible brand of the cross upon those who gave themselves to God. Confirmation bestowed the sign of Christ's proprietorship over each Christian.[7] As St. Cyril of Jerusalem said:

> Be sure not to regard chrism merely as ointment. Just as the bread of the eucharist after the invocation of the Holy Spirit is no longer just bread, but the body of Christ, so the holy chrism after the invocation is no longer ordinary ointment but Christ's grace, which through the present of the Holy Spirit instills . . . divinity into us.[8]

After the seal of confirmation was given, new Christians were welcomed into the community by participating in their first communion. On Easter morning, as part of the unified rites of initiation, new members were admitted to the Lord's table with great affection. Mark Searle writes:

> Then, for the first time, the newly baptized are permitted to join the faithful in their prayers and, afterward, to exchange the kiss of peace with them. The liturgy of the eucharist then begins and the newly baptized celebrate their incorporation into the body of Christ by sharing in Holy Communion. At long last, after perhaps as much as three years of association with the Church, they are allowed to celebrate and pray with the believing community. It is the climax of the whole process of conversion, and as a sign that they have arrived in the Promised Land, that they are given, besides the eucharistic bread and cup, a cup of milk mixed with honey, as well as a drink of water to signify the purification of the inner self.[9]

11

Again, we want to stress that the power of confirmation in the early church was primarily a consequence of the fact that it was part of the unified rites of Christian initiation. There was a clear synergy of water, oil, bread, and wine which drew their significance and power from one another. The joy of becoming Christian was portrayed through one grand liturgical pageant on Easter.

The fourth lesson the ancient church can teach us is that confirmation lost its power as it became separated from baptism and first communion. Many, including James White, suggest that what is most needed in our own time is a reunification of these rites:

> *Christian initiation ought to be complete on one occasion. We are not baptized into Christ's death and resurrection for only half way membership. Nor were we incorporated into the body of Christ with any reservations. Our welcome into the spirit-filled community is total. Therefore, the ancient practice of completing initiation on one occasion, especially at sunrise on Easter morning, seems unsurpassed. Anything that suggests that the Holy Spirit is divided between baptism and confirmation ought to be avoided. Thus, the new rites suggest baptism, laying-on of hands and first communion, all on one occasion.*[10]

Today the church continues to be hampered by the fragmentation of the rites of Christian initiation and the domestication of the sacraments. For many church members, baptism and Holy Communion have no power of transformation. Babies are politely sprinkled with water. Youth are routinely catechized a decade or more after their baptism through a process James White calls a "confirmation industry," but with no expectation that the seal of confirmation will (in the words of Cyril) "instill divinity" or result in the heightened commitment to the church we desire. The sacrament of Holy Communion continues to be disconnected from the experience of Christian initiation.

As we have already noted, if we wish for experiences that can excite the next generation about becoming Christian, we would do well to recreate the power of the unified rites of Christian initiation that played such a prominent role in the ancient community of faith.

But before we consider how the power of Christian initiation can be regained, we need to understand how it was lost. By exploring this question in greater detail we can achieve a clearer understanding of why confirmation in the modern era is so ✓ ineffective.

## FROM THE MIDDLE AGES TO THE REFORMATION TO TODAY

We have noted that the sacrament of confirmation began to lose its sense of place and purpose as early as the sixth century. During this era, confirmation became separated from baptism and Holy Communion. But why did this separation occur, and why did it continue through the Reformation and beyond?

By the sixth century, Christianity had become an established state religion, and the church grew rapidly. It soon became impossible for the bishop to confirm every newly baptized Christian by the laying-on of hands and anointing with chrism. Baptism occurred in so many churches on Easter Sunday that one person could not confirm them all, as had been the practice in earlier centuries. At the same time, the theology of St. Augustine was largely responsible for a radical growth in infant baptism. From the early sixth century on, the church began to baptize infants based upon Augustine's contention that any child who died unbaptized was unable to receive the gift of eternal life. Eventually, this view was legislated by secular authorities so that parents who failed to have their newborns promptly baptized could be punished by civil law.

With these two developments, the unified rites of Christian initiation began to break down. Baptism became less a matter of becoming Christian than of inoculating souls against eternal damnation. Baptisms began to be offered without preparation or personal decision, and although it was desired that a baptized child should be confirmed as soon as possible, the sheer number of baptized children insured that confirmation would be further delayed. As Mark Searle argues the separation between baptism, confirmation, and Holy Communion gave rise to speculative theologies that sought to describe each in exclusive ways:

> The church developed a fuller and more elaborate celebration of the
> original sacrament of Christian initiation so that it eventually
> came to take place in stages, but the stages retained their intel-
> ligibility as long as they were seen to be in strict continuity with
> one another, marking a single process of conversion and forma-
> tion. Once the stages began to be considered as units each having
> a separate and distinct significance, the temptation was to make a
> somewhat arbitrary allotment of meaning to each section.[11]

Confirmation was particularly vulnerable to a loss of meaning. As it was separated from baptism and communion the church was faced with a new theological challenge: how could the sacrament of confirmation retain its significance? One of the first to offer a new theology for confirmation was Faustus, a fourth-century bishop. Anticipating the need for confirmation to have its own distinctive role, Faustus suggested that confirmation's purpose was to strengthen Christians to do battle in the world. He wrote:

> So the Holy Spirit, who descended upon the baptismal waters
> bearing salvation, gave at the font all that is needed for innocence.
> At confirmation [the Spirit] gives an increase for grace, for in this
> world those who survive through the different stages of life, must
> walk among dangers and invisible enemies. In baptism we are
> born again to life, after baptism we are confirmed for battle. In
> baptism we are washed, after baptism we are strengthened.[12]

This perspective found favor among later generations of Christians who sought to make a case for the significance of confirmation after it was separated from baptism and first communion. But other theologians went even further by suggesting that confirmation perfected or completed baptism. The Council of Trent (1545–63) defined confirmation in the following way:

14

*To confirmation it is peculiarly given first to perfect the grace of*
*baptism; for those who have been made Christian by baptism still*
*have in some sort the tenderness and softness, as it were, of new-*
*born infants (1 Peter 2:2), and afterwards become, by the sacra-*
*ment of chrism, stronger against the assaults of the world, the*
*flesh, and the devil, and their mind is fully confirmed in faith to*
*confess and glorify the name of our Lord Jesus Christ, whence,*
*also, no doubt, originated the very name (of confirmation).*[13]

Despite the creation of such theologies, no single, compelling perspective about confirmation emerged. In the middle ages, the significance of confirmation was increasingly called into question, and intense theological debate occurred concerning the role confirmation might play in strengthening the faith of baptized Christians.

With the onset of the Protestant Reformation, more radical theological perspectives concerning the significance of confirmation appeared. The reformers charged that the purpose of confirmation as practiced in the Roman Catholic church was to glorify the role of bishops. For Luther, the suggestion that confirmation perfected baptism was specious. He asserted that baptism needed no perfection; it was whole and magnificent in its own right. Further, he denied that confirmation was a sacrament at all:

*Among these we see no reason for numbering confirmation. For*
*to constitute a sacrament there must be above all things else*
*a word of divine promise, by which faith must be exercised.*
*But we read nowhere that Christ ever gave a promise concerning*
*confirmation.*[14]

Luther believed that baptism was "the first sacrament and the foundation of all the others, without which none of the others can be received." Through baptism the grace of God was offered as a gift, and those who accepted it on faith were saved. Luther wrote in *The Babylonian Captivity of the Church*:

*Now, the first thing to be considered about baptism is the divine*
*promise, which says, "The one who believes and is baptized will be*

*saved" (Mark 16:16). This promise must be set far above all the glitter or works, vows, religious orders, and whatever else [humans have] introduced, for on it all our salvation depends. But we must so consider it as to exercise our faith in it, and have no doubt whatever that once we have been baptized, we are saved. For unless faith is present or is conferred in baptism, baptism will profit nothing.[15]*

Luther was concerned that Christians continually remember their baptism and believe in the promises of God's grace that they represented. For him, baptism was not fulfilled only in the moment when it was taking place, but as it was continually believed in the lives of Christians. To strengthen this understanding, Luther devised the Shorter Catechism to provide all baptized Christians—and especially youth—a concise explanation of the principal doctrines of the Reformed church. These were to be accepted on faith.

The publication and use of the Shorter Catechism had the effect of providing a new approach to confirmation. Rather than being a liturgical sacrament that sealed one's baptism, confirmation became an educational program through which one's belief in the saving power of baptism was strengthened. The Catechism was presented in the form of questions and answers so that the faithful might quickly grasp the essentials of Christian doctrine. After each commandment, article of faith, or sentence of prayer, the question was asked, "What does this mean?" The answer was always the personal testimony of a baptized Christian saved by faith. As Luther observed:

*For baptism is not a false sign. Neither does sin completely die, nor grace completely rise, until the sinful body that we carry about in this life is destroyed, as the Apostle says in the same passage (Rom. 6:6–7). For as long as we are in the flesh the desires of the flesh stir and are stirred. For this reason, as soon as we begin to believe, we also begin to die to this world and live to God in the life to come; so that faith is truly a death and a resurrection, that is, it is that spiritual baptism into which we are submerged and from which we rise.[16]*

16

We do not suggest that Luther intended his Shorter Catechism to become the prototype for an intellectual approach to confirmation, but this is in fact what has happened. Luther's catechetical approach is the model for the many modern Protestant educational programs prior to confirmation and for confirmation classes themselves.

Although Luther originally published the Shorter Catechism for families to use in strengthening faith around the supper table or hearth, subsequent generations saw in this resource a primer that could instill faith in youth. Soon it was being used in formal classroom situations to instruct young people to proclaim their belief in Jesus Christ. Those who participated in such programs of formal catechesis signaled their willingness to believe in the teachings of the church and, as Luther put it, "return to the power of your baptism . . . and do again what you were baptized to do and what your baptism signified." In *Luther's Works* we read:

> *Thus you see how rich a Christian is, that is, one who has been*
> *baptized! Even if [you] would, [you] could not lose [your] salva-*
> *tion, however much [you] sinned, unless [you] refused to believe.*
> *For no sin can condemn [you] save unbelief alone. All other sins,*
> *so long as the faith in God's promise made in baptism returns or*
> *remains, are immediately blotted out through that same faith, or*
> *rather through the truth of God, because he cannot deny himself if*
> *you confess him and faithfully cling to him in his promise.*[17]

A similar approach to confirmation was offered by John Calvin and the Reformed church tradition. Like other Protestant reformers, Calvin insisted that scripture recognized only two sacraments—Baptism and Holy Communion. The rest, Calvin said, "were empty show." Whereas Luther published a catechism to help believers rehearse their faith in the saving act of baptism, Calvin created his *Institutes* to fortify faith in God with knowledge of God. Roland Bainton notes:

> *Calvin's Institutes begin not with justification by faith [as in*
> *Luther's understanding] but with the knowledge of God. Calvin*
> *was in the tradition of those scholastics who declined to make faith*

17

*and knowledge mutually exclusive, insisting rather that they are*
*simply different modes of apprehension.*[18]

Education played a more important role in Calvin's theology than it did in Luther's. Education was the means by which one learned to submit to God's authority on the one hand and to live as one of the spiritually elect on the other. The curricula designed to achieve these goals were the Heidelberg Catechism and the Westminster Shorter Catechism. These became the standard means of catechetical instruction for the German Reformed Church in the United States and for the Reformed Church in America.

The major emphasis of this style of education was to offer a program by which doctrine is studied, memorized, accepted, and expressed. If baptism was the sacrament by which a Christian was reborn through the grace of God, confirmation was the process of catechetical study by which he or she learned to live as a Christian in the world. Again, Bainton writes:

> To this end, the Calvinists expended colossal energies in the ruling
> of cities, the converting of kingdoms, the beheading of a king, and
> the taming of wildernesses. Because they felt themselves to be the
> elect of God, they were fearless and indomitable. They worked
> with fury because they knew, that although history is long, life is
> short.[19]

The radical reform movement offered a third Protestant approach to catechesis. The Anabaptists believed that Christianity was a countercultural religion meant to exist apart from the mass of society and to bear witness to spiritual values that the world would never accept. Anabaptists practiced adult baptism because they believed that being Christian necessitated a personal choice for Christ and a commitment to follow the standards of the New Testament in an uncompromising way. In their view, the ministry of the church was not to baptize all infants in order to save their souls but to nurture a select community of believers who were prepared to take upon themselves the yoke of Christ. Their model for saying "yes" to faith through baptism had little to do with ritual transformation or with believing in baptism's saving power. Rather, the Anabaptists approached baptism as a commitment to live by the word of God and be a part of a Christian community that would rigorously live out biblical values. Catechesis became the means by which persons readied themselves to become members of Christ's church.

While the Protestant denominations did much to develop educational processes by which Christians could strengthen their faith, they—like the Catholics before them—largely failed to provide a unified rite of initiation that could connect baptism, confirmation, and Holy Communion, and reestablish the power of becoming Christian that was uniquely present in the early church. Only the Anabaptists provided this unity, and they did so by restricting baptism to adults.

We see, then, that there were many approaches to confirmation through the first sixteen centuries of the church's existence. Historically, it would be inaccurate to suggest that the Christian community has had a single theology of confirmation. It would be more appropriate to speak of theologies of confirmation which the church has developed to strengthen faith in the following ways:

**Early Catholic Church**
- Confirmation is the seal of baptism with holy oil.
- Confirmation strengthens faith through sacrament, rite, and ritual.

**Luther**
- Confirmation is a catechism designed to exercise our faith received in baptism.
- Confirmation strengthens faith through belief.

**Calvin**
- Confirmation is a catechism designed to teach us to live as the spiritually elect in the world.
- Confirmation strengthens faith through knowledge and initiation into the spiritually elect of the society.

### Radical Reformers

- In preparation for baptism confirmation teaches new believers to follow Christ.
- Such preparation strengthens faith through a decision to join the alternative community of the church and be baptized as an adult.

Given such a variety of interpretations, it is not surprising to note the majority of contemporary Christians are uncertain about the meaning of confirmation. Most continue to believe that it is important, as evidenced by the commitment parents have to ensuring that their youth participate in this rite, although they are not clear about what the experience is supposed to accomplish. As often as not, the impact of confirmation programs in our churches is compromised by conflicting expectations and contradictory goals. In autonomous denominations, such as the United Church of Christ, the diverse expectations are more paralyzing. Because there is no denominational norm for what becoming Christian means, many congregations create their own programs and confirm persons into their own communities of faith, but there is often little awareness that these young people are saying "yes" to their baptism into the universal body of Christ which exists in all times and places.

Granted that there is a need to clarify our vision about confirmation, what should confirmation be? How should it be reconnected to the sacraments of baptism and eucharist? When should confirmation occur? How long should it last? We will explore these issues in the next chapter.

### DISCUSSION QUESTIONS

1. What new things did you learn in this chapter about the history of confirmation in the Christian church?
2. Which parts of the history of confirmation most excites you? Which are most disappointing?
3. What are the most important things we as modern Christians need to learn from the history of confirmation in the Christian church?

4. If you could change three things about the way confirmation has evolved over the past two thousand years, what three changes would you make, and what effect would you hope those changes might have in the life of the church?
5. If you could reclaim three things about confirmation from earlier centuries in the church, what would they be?

## CHAPTER THREE

# What Should Confirmation Be Today?

We have noted that the majority of contemporary confirmation programs do not accomplish what they set out to do. We have also explored the historical roots of confirmation in order to understand its original significance and the reasons its power has been lost. Knowing these things, how do we re-imagine the rite of confirmation so that it strengthens faith and reestablishes the link between baptism and church membership?

We are proposing a new vision of confirmation with these three defining elements:

1. Confirmation should be rooted in the historic unity of baptism, confirmation, and Holy Communion.
2. Confirmation should be a repeatable rite of the church in which members say "yes" to their baptism by acknowledging faith-strengthening experiences throughout the course of their lives.
3. Confirmation should encourage the church to offer continual faith-forming experiences and repeatable rites of confirmation.

With these three defining elements in mind, we would like to explore each in greater detail.

1. Originally, confirmation was the sign and seal of baptism, and we suggest that confirmation return to be rooted in this original understanding in order to make it clear that baptism is

23

the sacrament that makes persons Christian. This can be done by reuniting baptism, confirmation, and Holy Communion so that the sacrament of baptism, whether done for very young children, youth, or adults, includes the ritual act of confirmation.

Many recent liturgies compiled for worship in the historic Protestant denominations have already recovered this unity. For example, in the *Book of Worship* of the United Church of Christ, we find the following ritual accompanying the administering of water in the service of baptism:

> The pastor may lay hands on the head of the baptized and say
> these or similar words. "The Holy Spirit be upon you,
> _____, child of God, disciple of Christ, member of
> the church.[1]

In the earliest Christian tradition, as we have noted, the symbolic acts for confirmation were the laying-on of hands and anointing with consecrated oil. Through baptism children, youth, and adults were welcomed into membership in Christ's body, the church. Through confirmation, this welcome was sealed and consecrated. In our view, the United Church of Christ *Book of Worship* seeks to recover this historic connection between baptism and confirmation—a goal that we commend.

We would like fully to recapture the unified rites of initiation by suggesting that first communion should also accompany the sacrament of baptism and rite of confirmation. For infants, communion would involve moistening the lips with wine or grape juice and a bit of bread. This part of the service of Christian initiation is a traditional one, with its roots in the ancient church.

2. Confirmation should be a repeatable rite of the church in which the entire community says "yes" to faith-strengthening experiences at various times during the course of members' lives. We need to recognize that confirming moments not only occur during the teenage years but at other times in the lives of Christians. At all such moments, the church needs to offer children, adolescents, and adults the opportunity to say "yes" to their baptism and be confirmed by the community of faith of which they are a part.

24

3. Our vision of confirmation encourages the church continually to offer faith-forming experiences which may culminate in the repeatable rite of confirmation. As we provide these faith forming opportunities, we need to be careful not to fall into the trap of believing that educational programs are synonymous with confirmation. We should offer faith-forming educational experiences which can lead persons to choose to participate in the rite of confirmation. We suggest that it would be helpful to call the educational programs "faith formation" rather than "confirmation." We hope for a lifelong process of faith-forming experiences that can be celebrated in our congregations. Some of these may occur as a result of formal educational programs, but others will be a consequence of life experiences which the church can acknowledge as formative. In either case, we offer the vision of faith-forming education in the belief that it will lead persons to participate in repeatable rites of confirmation. The repeatable rite of confirmation needs to be a flexible and powerful one which celebrates many different experiences of God in the lives of children, youth, and adults. On both educational and ritual levels, the church needs to be prepared to identify many different faith-strengthening events in the lives of Christians and help them to affirm their baptism through repeatable rites of confirmation.

Do repeatable rites of confirmation *confer* faith-strengthening to the recipient or do they *recognize* that such strengthening has already occurred? In our vision, the rite acts in both capacities. Confirmation strengthens faith in a number of ways. It initially serves as the sign of baptism. It formally articulates that baptism makes one a member of the church of Jesus Christ and challenges Christians to live out their baptism. It ritually commemorates the grace of God in members' lives. Finally, it provides ongoing opportunities for Christians to participate in faith-forming education. Confirmation also recognizes other ways in which faith is strengthened. It serves as a rite that celebrates the many ways in which Christians have found new meaning, empowerment, healing, or transformation in their faith.

With this holistic vision of confirmation in mind, let us examine how we have reduced the rite of confirmation to a series of

25

educational programs for youth. By evaluating the strengths and weakness of our current practice, we can discover productive ways to move toward a new approach.

We have noted that the commitment of grass-roots Christians to teenage confirmation programs is profound. Few other contemporary rites and rituals in the life of congregations engender the same degree of loyalty, support, and participation. Most members of our churches expect teenagers to be confirmed by the church just as strongly as they desire baptism for infants or funeral services for the deceased. For most members, confirmation is a gut level concern. Without a formal confirmation program, members seem instinctively to feel as if something is missing in the faith formation of youth.

Contemporary motivations for confirmation are complex. We propose that there are at least five core reasons why Christians believe that confirmation for young people is an indispensable rite. Depending upon one's background of faith, any or all of these concerns may be determinative.

## 1. COMPLETION OF BAPTISM

This first motivation is a carry-over from medieval theology. It postulates that confirmation is a "perfection" or "completion" of infant baptism. In this view, a confirmation rite, held many years after one's baptism, bestows a final blessing grace upon young people.

The operative assumption in this interpretation is that baptism requires a supplementary rite in order to be complete. That which was begun through baptism must be completed through confirmation.

For many church members, sending youth into the world without the official stamp of confirmation is the religious equivalent of sending children to school without complete vaccinations. As children need a full series of treatments to build up immunity to polio, many Christians believe teenagers need a full set of inoculations of God's grace in order to cope with an uncertain world. In this view, confirmation provides emotional reassurance to adults that they have done their best to prepare their youth to rely upon God as they assume an adult role in a society. Unfortunately, many confirmation programs cause teenagers to build up more of an immunity to Christian faith than to the temptations of the world.

We believe this is the single most unproductive approach to confirmation now practiced in the church. As Luther noted, the sacrament of baptism needs nothing to make it complete. In baptism, we are fully reborn through God's grace and unconditionally welcomed into the church. Confirmation, done as part of the baptismal liturgy, provides a powerful sign and seal to the power of the baptismal event. Repeated acts of confirmation can serve as liturgical benchmarks when faith is strengthened.

Throughout the unfolding of our lives, we should expect to be claimed by many moments in which our faith is transformed or strengthened. It is appropriate that confirmation be used by the church to bless these special times. Instead of limiting confirmation to an experience for youth, we propose that the church be a place where faith-forming experiences are confirmed at every age and stage of life.

## 2. CONCERN FOR DEVELOPMENT OF PERSONAL FAITH

The importance of confirmation is also related to the concerns many church members have for the destiny of the souls of children. In the preceding chapter, we noted Augustine's contention that unbaptized children cannot be saved and pointed out that much of the motivation for infant baptism is a consequence of parental concern that their children's sins be expiated by every means possible.

In churches that encourage infant baptism, adult members often view this sacrament as an act of divine protection. They assume responsibility for baptizing young ones into the community of faith because they believe that, through baptism, Christians inherit eternal life: "The one who believes and is baptized will be saved" (Mark 16:16). But infant baptism does not involve assent. Although it is a sacrament based upon grace, it is done for infants rather than being the product of their own choice.

Because many adults worried whether their own commitment to baptize their children would be sufficient to pass on faith, they decided that a final educational program was needed to allow youth to give assent to their baptism. Confirmation eventually filled this need by becoming a time for youth to participate in an educational program, approach the Christian faith with the aid of reason, give assent to their baptism, and believe in its saving power.

Many Christians seem to doubt that the grace offered during infant baptism is sufficient for salvation. Instead they believe that an adult affirmation of belief must eventually supplement the gift of infant baptism if it is to "take" and have a saving effect on the lives of those who are baptized. Because of these beliefs, confirmation is the means by which adults in the faith community seek to offer children the opportunity to affirm their own baptism by confessing their faith in Jesus Christ. Such a confession of faith, it is hoped, will lead young people to embrace the church that first baptized them.

Unfortunately, confirmation often has the opposite effect. As we noted previously, well over half of those who have participated in confirmation programs since the 1960s in historic protestant denominations have dropped out of the faith community.

## 3. SEARCHING FOR A COMPELLING VISION OF GOD

The third motivation for confirmation is the desire of adults to share their love of God with children in the church. Many who desire a strong confirmation education program hope that meaningful church participation during the teenage years will offer youth an opportunity to discover a personal relationship with God. Those adults seek to provide a supportive community in which confirmands can dialogue with adults about the nature of the spiritual journey. They seek to offer opportunities for youth to express their relationship with God in service to the world. John

28

Westerhoff described this approach in *Will Our Children Have Faith?*:

> *The most profound questions of life have no answers; each only opens new questions that lead even deeper into the mystery of [life] and ultimately to the mystery of God. What our children are really asking is for us to reveal and share ourselves and our faith, not to provide dogmatic answers. We do not need to answer our children's questions, but we do need to make our faith available to them as a source for their learning and growth. We can offer our own experiences, doubts and fears, questions, insights and stories. We can say to them, "I don't know the answer, but I will help you search." "I just don't know how to explain it, but together we might discover some insight." You see, it is in the relationship be- tween us during our shared quest that God is revealed.*[2]

Young people need the opportunity to probe the uncertain and mysterious territory of faith. Adults hope that youth will find in the church a faith-formation program that illuminates the reality of God. The best youth ministries offer such experiences. A Connecticut youth group engages in multicultural education with youth in Puerto Rico. A confirmation class in Minnesota journeys to work with Habitat for Humanity in Appalachia. A Rocky Mountain confirmation class spends a week together in the wilderness as a community of faith. In each of these cases, experiences of community are shared, questions of faith asked, and the Christian faith celebrated. In the midst of relationships and deep sharing about what it means to be faithful, God is revealed to participants.

We applaud these programs as helpful and as faith trans- forming for youth. Ultimately, however, faith formation is limited and restricted by focusing all the hopes of confirmation upon youth. Children also need to be encouraged to know God, and adults need opportunities to strengthen their faith by confronting vital questions of identity, relationships, vocation, meaning, and lifestyle. A lifelong process of confirmation would provide the opportunity for all of these experiences of faith to be blessed by the church.

## 4. CHOOSING AN ETHIC THAT AFFIRMS LIFE

Adults in the church want to provide enduring values to their children. The modern world is intensely egotistical and materialistic. The dominant values of our society seem to be based upon one's freedom to gratify the self. A popular bumper sticker reads: "We're spending our children's inheritance." It sometimes seems as if the society in which we live has been reduced to a collection of individuals who pursue personal happiness while trying to convince themselves that they owe nothing to others or to the future. This naked pursuit of self-interest and the inevitable neglect of the common good has compromised the integrity of every major social institution in our society. Television evangelists have exploited the pastoral office for personal gain, bankers have misused public funds, and politicians have engaged in unethical conduct. Healthy role models are lacking.

As our young people grow up in such a society, adults long for them to be exposed to traditional faith values such as justice, peace, compassion, and servanthood. To many youth, these words seem as puzzling as a foreign language. More often than not, youth reject basic Christian values as impractical. Many are attracted to power, success,wealth, and pleasure—the worldly priorities that are commended to them by those in the public limelight. The wisdom of contemporary culture teaches youth a great deal about how to get what they want but little about their place in the scheme of things.

The church can offer an alternative to our culture's emphasis upon personal achievement and gratification. At its best, the church provides a unique source of meaning in our society because it transmits enduring values. Many in the church long for a ministry that will communicate these deeper faith teachings to youth. Parents hope that confirmation will be the program in which such education occurs. When adults encourage youth to participate in the church's faith-formation programs, they do so with the same commitment as the authors of Proverbs, who sought to teach their children wisdom:

30

*My child, do not forget my teaching,*
*but let your heart keep my commandments;*
*for length of days and years of life*
*and abundant welfare they will give you. (Prov. 3:1–2)*

We applaud this goal. It is one that can empower the faith of youth. But if confirmation is nothing more than ethical instruction, the rite loses its faith dimension. Without connecting confirmation to a relationship with God, we run the risk of communicating to youth that one becomes ethical merely by understanding certain ideas and principles. Nothing could be further from the truth. To be a guiding force in one's life, ethical thinking and action must be encouraged, not just during the teenage years, but as a lifelong process. Moreover, Christians of all ages need opportunities to strengthen their faith by allowing God to inform their ethical base. Christian faith is not merely a product of the values people of faith choose to make their own; it is also a result of God's grace guiding us to a deeper way of perceiving the world. The church needs to teach the faith disciplines that help people to discern God's way.

## 5. THE JOY OF COMMUNITY AND COMMON LIFE

The church can be a special place when it prioritizes the sharing of lives. In the church, we want to be present to one another in ways that are accepting, helpful, loving, and healing. The church reminds us that we cannot discover meaning in life by ourselves or for ourselves. To be sure, there is value to be found in our individual journeys of faith. Personal spiritual disciplines such as silence, prayer, and reflection help us to know ourselves and develop a relationship with God. But self-knowledge and personal love of God are incomplete. To experience abundant life we also need to share our lives with others and receive their care. Most adults are active in a church because in some way they have been loved and cared for by a community of believers. Such experiences happen in the church all the time.

31

A woman returns to her hometown because of the untimely death of her father. She feels a sense of grief at his death but, even more, she feels guilty because she did not spend his last days with him. The pastor visits with the woman and understands her feelings of guilt. He shares the times when he visited with her father and explains the things her father said before his death. He lets her know her father loved her and was proud of her. The pastor and the woman share a prayer together. Tears are shed. As the pastor leaves, the woman says, "I want to thank you for being here for me today. It feels so good to be able to share my feelings and to have them understood and accepted."

A youth group is having a retreat. The members are sharing their experiences of relationships in the group. Two girls express their concern about being shut out of the group. Other youth begin to respond. One has a hard time accepting the feelings of the two girls who are feeling excluded. "Nobody's trying to shut you out," he says. Another reaches out to the two girls who feel shut out. "I'm sorry you feel excluded. You're a really important part of the group and I'm glad you're here." Gradually, everyone feels heard, and the walls between "in" and "out" groups begin to disappear. The youth advisors invite the members to join in a prayer and a group hug. Although painful in the early stages, the evening ends with a feeling of mutual understanding, acceptance, and trust. Everyone experiences the church's claim that God dwells with the gathered community in a special way and bonds them together in love.

A ninety-year-old church member is able to live independently, but she wishes she could still garden and plant some flowers. A lay care-giver hears about her situation and volunteers to help her put in and care for a garden.

Such moments make the church a confirming community. When children attend the church, we hope they will experience the meaning that comes from caring for and being cared about by others. Confirmation programs have been the major events which adult members hope will offer teenagers powerful experiences of community that will carry over into adult life.

It is good to offer youth intense experiences of Christian community, but as the illustrations above point out, youth are not the only people who need connections with others. We need a broad process of nurture that offers the joy of a caring community to all ages in the church, providing opportunities for people to confirm their faith with other Christians at various stages of their lives. We suggest that confirmation for youth should not be the only major experience of community-building in the lives of Christians, but rather just one among many important experiences of life together.

These are the five core motivations for confirmation in our time. They represent the profound yearnings of adults in the church. As we have pointed out, however, not all motivations provide an adequate basis for renewing the rite of confirmation in our time. A new vision of confirmation must balance two very difficult tasks. On the one hand, it must meet the diverse motivations of Christians who want to pass on faith to the next generation. On the other hand, a new vision of confirmation needs to interpret the rite clearly. These diverse hopes make it difficult to offer a rite that is both well-focused and inclusive. How can we achieve more clarity about confirmation while also seeking to meet the diverse needs of our members?

In the first place, it is helpful to remember that in the Reformed church tradition, confirmation has been understood as a rite rather than a sacrament. Traditionally, all sacraments are understood to be rites of the church, but not all rites are sacraments. Rites, as J. G. Davies notes, are formal acts that "constitute a religious observance."[3] They are based upon human actions that seek to, "facilitate [our] contact with the holy in such a way that [we] may be preserved and at the same time enter in to a relationship with the source of [our] being."[4]

Sacraments also seek to connect persons with the holy, but they do so in the assurance that Christ has promised that these human actions are specifically ordained by God as having faith-strengthening character. We might say that sacraments empower members of the church because of what God promises to do for us. Rites that are nonsacramental empower members through what we hope to do in response to God. The two Protestant sacraments, baptism and Holy Communion, are taken to be outward and visible signs of an inward grace offered by Christ to all generations of the faithful. Through baptism and the eucharist, we are explicitly promised in scripture that we will be transformed and renewed by the action of the Holy Spirit upon us. By distinction, a rite of the church serves to create a context in which to be receptive to the leading of the Holy Spirit in our lives.

In the Protestant tradition, sacraments have been held by the church to be more fundamental than rites. The two sacraments flow from Christ's life, teaching, and ministry, and they are ordained by him in scripture as a means of spiritual rebirth and new life. Reformation theologians have argued that rites, while also important, do not possess this same explicit, transforming power. In the rite of marriage, for instance, we do not experience the same sort of outward and visible sign of an inward spiritual grace that is discovered in bread and wine. Rather, the rite of marriage is an occasion when a couple seek for God's blessing in the creating of a vowed relationship. The sacrament of Holy Communion can be included in the rite of marriage specifically to include the unique sacramental presence of the risen Christ.

Many Roman Catholic theologians have criticized confirmation through the years as a "sacrament in search of a theology." We would suggest that the current Protestant challenge is to discover a theology of confirmation that helps confirmation to regain its integrity as a significant rite of the church. Such a theology needs to avoid the temptation to try to make confirmation more than it can be. It seems important to recall that confirmation grew out of a rich initiation ritual which was originally very simple: a prayer offered by the bishop with hands extended over the newly baptized Christian's head and the anointing of the initiate with chrism. Confirmation was then followed by first communion.

We believe that the significance of the rite of confirmation is dependent upon its connection to the sacraments of baptism and Holy Communion. If we want a definitive theology of confirma-

34

tion that clarifies its meaning as a rite of the church, that theology needs to portray confirmation in the context of its relationship to water, bread, and cup.

We once again emphasize that the golden age of Christian initiation occurred during the first five centuries of the church, when one unified rite of belonging was the norm. The purpose of this unified rite (as the Roman Catholic general introduction to the contemporary rites of Christian initiation says) is to cause people to experience a spiritual rebirth:

> *Through the sacraments of Christian initiation men and women are freed from the power of darkness. With Christ they die, and are buried and rise again. They receive the Spirit of adoption which makes them God's sons and daughters and, with the entire people of God, they celebrate the memorial of the Lord's death and resurrection.*[5]

An experience that promises such a profound personal transformation can only be adequately ritualized by recovering the early church's uniquely powerful liturgy of initiation. There are two ways to reconnect baptism, confirmation, and eucharist in the liturgical life of our churches.

One way to offer the unified rites of initiation is to return to the practice of adult baptism as it was practiced in the early Christian church and in some branches of the Reformation churches today. If we were to adopt this approach, youth in the congregation would submit themselves to intense catechetical preparation and would have to choose to become Christian by being baptized and confirmed into the community of faith. As Tertullian proscribed: "Let them be made Christians when they have become competent to know Christ."

There are several advantages to this alternative. Adult baptism that follows a period of catechesis makes the process of becoming Christian a powerful individual decision. Such a process can make committed Christians. In this model, baptism is the culmination of Christian initiation rather than its introduction, and confirmation plays a critical supplementary role, both educationally and liturgically.

In this approach, confirmation becomes the process of first understanding Christian faith and then signing and sealing one's baptism. Rather than being perceived as the completion of baptism (which, as we have seen, loads an impossible burden upon the rite which it was never meant to carry), confirmation is the means by which one prepares for and acknowledges death, burial, and rebirth in the spirit of Jesus Christ.

A second way to reconnect baptism, confirmation, and Holy Communion is through unified rites of initiation for persons of *all* ages, including infants and children. There are also some attractive strengths in this model. First among these strengths is the attention and honor given to children in the community of faith. Infant baptism offers the community the special opportunity to welcome, bless and sanctify each new life. The significance of infant baptism should not be underestimated. What most fundamentally occurs is the bestowing of the gift of the Holy Spirit upon new children of God. It is a celebration of Emmanuel— "God is with us!"—and a sign that God is an indwelling Creator who offers all generations the miracle of intimate personal relationship.

Infant baptism opens the community of faith to God's grace in a special way. When we behold the presentation of a vulnerable, innocent baby and participate in the joyful liturgy of her or his Christian initiation, we remember that God's love is a gift of grace freely given to all individuals who become part of the body of Christ.

When we compare the strengths and weaknesses of adult and infant baptism, we discover that there are compelling theological reasons for baptizing the very young. When we combine these theological reasons with the awareness that infant baptism is the most well established sacrament in the Reformation Protestant churches, the case for continuing Christian initiation shortly after birth is persuasive. But if we wish to retain infant baptism and link confirmation to it in order to recapture the integrity of the early church's rite of initiation, how shall we practice confirmation?

As we have suggested, what is needed is a return to the

practice of the early church, which combined baptism with the laying-on of hands and anointing with chrism. In this rite of initiation, confirmation is the seal which summarizes baptism just as an "amen" finalizes a prayer. The Orthodox scholar, Alexander Schmemann, offers a helpful understanding when he suggests that confirmation plays the role of personalizing the gift of grace received in baptism:

> In baptism [the baptized person] received the new life and was introduced into the realm of Incarnation, of the new nature. Now, he [or she] has received [a] unique personality, personal life, to be personally a living member of the body, a witness to Christ, a [child] of God, a partaker in the "royal priesthood" of the church.[6]

It needs to be said again that baptism is not a sacrament with something missing, nor does baptism depend upon confirmation for a "second" dose of grace. Rather, confirmation is the response of the people to God's transforming grace. The laying-on of hands and anointing are the signs that the community recognizes as the coming of the Holy Spirit into a new life in its midst. These acts also symbolize the willingness of all members of the church to nurture the newly baptized infant in the way of Christ.

There is more: the traditional unified rites of initiation also involved the eucharist. This was done because it was believed that each new member of the body of Christ was entitled to God's own special nurture in the community of faith. Originally, communion was a natural consequence of baptism.

At the altar of the Great Vigil of Easter, some who were baptized into the early church were given not only bread and wine, but also two extra cups, one filled with milk and honey and the other with water. The water was symbolic of the baptism of the inner person, and the milk and honey were signs of the promised land of the realm of God in which "they who believe are nurtured like little children." Nearly three centuries after the time of Hippolytus (who recorded the earliest rites of Christian initiation), the custom of offering the newly baptized a cup of milk and honey continued in the church at Rome. As infant baptism became the norm, the newly baptized continued to be served communion at the church in Rome. In the seventh century, the following description of infant communion was offered:

> After baptism and confirmation they go into mass and all of the infants receive communion. Care is to be taken lest after they have been baptized they receive any food of suckling before they communicate.[7]

The eucharist was understood to be the fundamental source of nurture of an infant spiritually reborn into the Christian community. Thus, no earthly food was to be given until after the newly baptized had received first communion. Usually, this first communion was received from the finger of the priest or presiding liturgist. This practice continued through the first twelve centuries of the church's life, making it a remarkably consistent liturgical tradition. In the Middle Ages, this traditional practice ceased. A strong pietistic movement developed through which the priesthood took custody of the eucharist to safeguard its holiness. Roland Bainton writes that the church "restricted the cup to the priest lest the clumsy laity should spill any of the blood of God." James White observed that "growing scrupulousness about the consecrated wine in twelfth-century piety led to the withholding of the chalice from laity of whatever age." Mark Searle offers a bit more biting analysis:

> When infant communion finally died out in the twelfth century . . . this was due less to any fear of irreverence than to the fact that the laity rarely received Holy Communion anyway.[8]

The Protestant reformers encouraged the separation of baptism and communion in their own fashion. Again, James White provides us with a useful insight:

> The tendency in Western Christianity for many centuries has been to limit the eucharist to adults and to expect the child to have progressed toward conceptual understanding of Christianity before being admitted to the Lord's table. In making confirmation, or public profession of faith necessary before receiving communion, the Reformation was only drawing to its logical conclusion a long course of development in the late medieval West. . . . [But] those

*who advocate infant baptism rarely realize that they undercut
their case when they baptize children and then decline to give them
communion until they are "ready" for it. Usually that means
when they reach "the age of reason," as if their communicant status were contingent upon being able to profess faith conceptually.[9]*

As we have also suggested, White goes on to call for a
reunification of baptism, confirmation, and communion:

*There is tendency to reunite the rites of initiation so that some
churches in the west are recovering the practice of infant baptism,
infant confirmation and infant communion all at the same occasion. One can hardly bar baptized children from the Lord's table
without questioning their baptism itself. If they have been united
to Christ and incorporated into the church through baptism, one
can hardly say that sharing in Christ's death and resurrection do
not quite count until they can understand it. What God does in
baptism for infants or for adults is not done halfway. It is a lifelong gift that places us within the priestly body. . . . We have not
wished to make baptism contingent upon actual faith in the case of
infants; no more do we wish to make the eucharist contingent
upon rational ability to explicate faith. Neither sacrament is a re-
ward for faith but a means to its development.[10]*

To regain its status as a significant rite of the church, confirmation needs to be reconnected to baptism and first communion.
In this way, it can clearly be included in the experience of becoming Christian. To do this is not difficult; we merely need to return
to the traditional rites of initiation that involved a laying-on of
hands and anointing with chrism after baptism. Through this
simple liturgical action, those who receive the gift of spiritual
rebirth in baptism are also confirmed through the giving of the
seal of the Holy Spirit.

In order to reestablish the rite of confirmation we suggest
that two specific actions be taken:

1. The sacrament of Holy Baptism should be connected to
   confirmation through the laying-on of hands and anointing the newly baptized Christian with oil.

39

2. First communion should be included in the rite of Christian initiation.

In the liturgy for initiation for children, we suggest that, following the baptism with water, a laying-on of hands and optional anointing with oil be offered. The pastor would then dismiss the parents, godparents, and other family members because the sacrament of baptism and rite of confirmation have been completed. Then the liturgy would proceed to the service of Holy Communion, which the newly baptized infant would be the first to celebrate. As in ancient days, she or he would be served the wine on the finger of the pastor or on a spoon. In this way, the contemporary Protestant church could reunite the rites of Christian initiation and bond persons to the church in a more dramatic way. In the process, the purpose of confirmation would be clarified and its place as an essential rite of the church enriched.

Dramatic, powerful rites of belonging are important to the church in our time. Many hunger for ritual that connects and bonds, not in a sentimental way, but with sincerity. Unified rites of Christian initiation that offer an experience of awe and wonder would be welcomed. We agree with Tom Driver's assessment that Christian ritual can provide a bridge between the realm of God and the world. He writes:

> The Christian life is characterized by the frequent crossing of a threshold between the practicalities of working for freedom in the historical world and the magic of the performance of freedom in the sacramental community. Neither mode of performance is sufficient alone.[11]

The power of Christian ritual lies in its capacity to offer a space for the experience of freedom in God's realm. Baptism, confirmation, and first communion can communicate that something grand is occurring in the heart, mind, and soul of Christians. To the extent they embody these experiences, the liturgies of the modern church (as in ancient days) can provide a deep sense awe and a profound experience of community.

A major goal of the rites of Christian initiation is to awaken the memories of all who participate in worship. Memories can be powerful as they often involve recalling one's own baptism or meaningful moments when others became a part of the church. Memories inevitably remind Christians of the mystery, majesty, and tradition of our faith.

Memories challenge Christians to remember that each generation of confirmed Christians expands the body of Christ. The body of Christ is dynamic. It is comprised both of spiritual ancestors who have lived and then died and of the present generation of believers. Those who are physically present in the church in any particular generation cannot forget their fathers and mothers of faith, for each living Christian is continually surrounded by "a great cloud of witnesses" whose legacy continues to influence the community of faith. By remembering our baptism and confirmation, we are led to honor those who transmitted the faith to us.

The apocryphal book *Ecclesiasticus* offers us a stirring example of the way that memory leads us to honor our ancestors in this way:

> Let us now praise famous men and women and our mothers and
> fathers in their generations.
> God apportioned to them great glory, majesty from the beginning.
> There were those who were rulers and were renowned for their
> power, giving counsel through their understanding and
> proclaiming prophecies.
> Leaders of the people in their deliberations and in understanding
> of learning for the people, wise in their words of instruction;
> Those who composed musical tunes, and set forth verses in
> writing;
> Rich persons furnished with resources, living peaceably in their
> habitations—
> All these were honored in their generations and were the glory of
> their times.
> There are some who have left a name so that the community
> proclaims their praise.
> And there are some who have no memorial, who have perished as
> though they had not been born. . . .
> But these were people of mercy, whose righteous deeds have not

41

*been forgotten; their prosperity will remain with their descendants, and their inheritance to their children's children.*

*Their posterity will continue for ever, and their glory will not be blotted out.*

*Their bodies were buried in peace, and their names live to all generations.*

*People will declare their wisdom, and the congregation proclaims their praise. (Ecclesiasticus 44:1–15)*

Memories of baptism and confirmation also inspire us to hope for the future. When we recall the baptism of children or adults, we remember how members prayed for God to fulfill their future, and we picture them being reborn through water and then confirmed with the seal of the Holy Spirit. These memories strengthen our belief in the grace of God and quicken our conviction that life has meaning and purpose. Through our memories of baptism and confirmation, we are stimulated to see within the life of each Christian gifts waiting to be awakened and dreams waiting to be expressed. As we are filled with these rich recollections, we find ourselves praying that God will bless the next generation.

Finally, Holy Communion reminds us of the ways we have been fed by God. When linked with our recollections of baptism and confirmation, these memories of bread and wine fill us with the knowledge that we are cared for, guided, and embraced by the love of God. If baptism, confirmation, and eucharist were reconsolidated into a unified rite of initiation, they would invoke these powerful associations. We need such unified rites of initiation to connect the worshiping community with the power resident in God's guidance of Christians in the world. Our members need help to deepen their awareness of what is occurring when they claim Jesus Christ as Lord. They need encouragement to develop an expectation that God transforms lives. We challenge readers to consider how they can help members of their congregations lose themselves in the unfolding drama of God's love. The following description of unified rites in the ancient church gives us an example of the power we might seek to experience through rites of initiation that expect transformation:

> "As soon as you come out of the font, you put on a dazzling gar-
> ment of pure white. This is a sign to the world of shining splendor
> and the way of life to which you have already passed in symbol,"
> writes Theodore of Mopsuestia. Just as the apostles were given a
> glimpse of the glory of Christ when they saw him transfigured,
> "and his face shone like the sun, and his garments became as white
> as light" (Matt. 17:2), so now the newly baptized, dressed in pure
> white, their faces glistening with oil, catch a glimpse of their own
> future transfiguration, when the time comes for them to take their
> place in that innumerable multitude of people "from every nation,
> from all tribes and peoples and tongues, standing before the throne
> and before the lamb, clothed in white robes, with palm branches in
> their hands," (Revelation 7:9). At the baptismal vigil of Easter, the
> newly baptized would be led into the church where the community
> was assembled and where the faithful had been occupied with
> prayer on their behalf. One can imagine the impact of their ar-
> rival: these figures who had been on the fringe of the community
> for so long, now being brought into its midst with shining robes.
> In the East, the community would strike up a chant, greeting
> them in the words of Paul: "In Christ Jesus you are all sons of God
> through faith. For many of you as were baptized into Christ have
> put on Christ. Alleluia!"[12]

We have seen that the primary way confirmation will gain theological meaning is for it to be a part of unified rites of initiation that cause persons to be "born from above" as members of the body of Christ. The role of confirmation is to help place Christians in an alternative community which can interpret the world for them in ways fundamentally different from those who have not been baptized and confirmed into the church. Unified rites of baptism, confirmation, and Holy Communion can inspire Christians to live with the tension between day-to-day life in a secular culture and the vision of faith taught by the church.

Baptism, confirmation, and first communion need to prepare

us to live life differently. The unified rite of Christian initiation is not meant to be a final act, however, but an introduction to a new way of life that requires continual encouragement.

In the next chapter we will explore how repeatable rites of confirmation can empower Christians to live out their baptism.

## DISCUSSION QUESTIONS

1. What is your reaction to our proposals concerning what confirmation should be today?
2. Which proposals seemed to be most meaningful for your church?
3. Which proposals would you most like to see enacted in your church, and what strategies might help that to happen?
4. Which proposals in this chapter were the most difficult for you to consider? What was the source of your difficulty?
5. What additional understandings of what confirmation should be today would you like to invite the authors to address?


Dear Ken and Peter:

To continue the conversation about confirmation, please address these concerns and ideas when exploring what confirmation should be today:

1.
2.
3.

Mail your ideas to:
R. Kenneth Ostermiller
320 South Maple Ave.
Greensburg, PA 15601

## CHAPTER FOUR

# Making Confirmation a Repeatable Rite

We have seen that the goal of unified rites of Christian initiation is to transform a secular way of life into one that is informed by spiritual possibility. In the process of this transformation, baptism and confirmation usher us from the world that *was* before our spiritual rebirth to the reign of God that *shall be*.

Initiation into Christian faith not only needs to transform us; it must also sustain us as we seek to live in the tension between worldly reality and the spiritual realm that has claimed us. Ideally, confirmation should not only seal our baptism, but also help us to live it out in light of the challenge given by the apostle Paul: "Be not conformed to the world, but transformed by the renewal of your minds so that you might prove what is the will of God" (Rom. 12:2).

Although baptism is the definitive moment during which persons are reborn in the power of the Holy Spirit, this transforming sacrament needs to be seen in a lifelong perspective. Luther rightly pointed out that "baptism is in force all through life" because it contains the promise of the continuing empowerment of the Holy Spirit. Baptism, then, is a dynamic sacrament. But, as powerful as it is, baptism needs the process of confirmation to provide liturgical and educational opportunities through which Christians can live out the promises God has offered them through water and the Word.

The *Book of Worship* in the United Church of Christ implicitly connects baptism to the original liturgical practice of confirmation so that the integrity of the unified rites of initiation in the early church is remembered and maintained.

In the *Book of Worship*, baptism is understood to be the sacrament by which "a person is incorporated into the universal church."[1] By distinction, confirmation is the rite by which Christians "give public assent to the baptismal promises"[2] made by the community of faith that originally witnessed the confirmand's baptism, including parents or sponsors. What is critical to acknowledge is the fact that baptism is the sacrament by which persons become Christian. Confirmation is the rite by which the community of faith and baptized Christians say "yes" to the miracle of rebirth in Christ through water and the Word.

Significantly, the *Book of Worship* also contains the rubric of the ancient church's original act of confirmation in the Order for Baptism. After the administering of water, the pastor is encouraged to lay hands on the head of the baptized and say: "The Holy Spirit be upon you, (name), child of God, disciple of Christ, member of the church."[3]

This laying-on of hands and formal prayer of consecration, as we have seen, *represents* the uniting of baptism with the church's earliest understanding of confirmation. The *Book of Worship*, therefore, encourages an implicit, unified rite of initiation through which one is born again of water and the Holy Spirit and then confirmed by the laying-on of hands and prayers. Through this act, the entire church confirms the moment of spiritual rebirth and prepares itself for that which will come when the infant will later affirm her or his baptism. Through the laying-on of hands and the prayer of the Holy Spirit, the pastor seals the baptism, and the congregation, parents, and sponsors affirm their willingness to be spiritual guides for the initiate and educate her or him into the mysteries of the Christian life.

In addition, "The Great Vigil of Easter" liturgy in the *Book of Worship* provides for the "Renewal of Baptismal Vows." Instructions for this part of the liturgy read as follows:

*The following creed in question form; a full creed, statement of
faith, or covenant; or another form prepared for the occasion may
be used. The questions are addressed to the congregation as individuals for affirmation of each person's baptism.*

LEADER: Do you reaffirm your renunciation of evil
and renew your commitment to Jesus Christ?

PEOPLE: I do.

LEADER: Do you believe in God?

PEOPLE: I believe in God, the creator of heaven and
earth.

LEADER: Do you believe in Jesus Christ?

PEOPLE: I believe in Jesus Christ, the only one begot-
ten of God before all worlds.

LEADER: Do you believe in the Holy Spirit?

PEOPLE: I believe in God, the Holy Spirit.

LEADER: Will you continue in the apostles' teaching
and community, in the breaking of bread and in prayer?

PEOPLE: I will, with God's help.

LEADER: Will you strive for justice and peace among
all people respecting the dignity of every human being?

PEOPLE: I will, with God's help. All who are able may
stand. In these or similar words, a leader may invoke God's
blessing upon all who have renewed their vows.

LEADER: Let us pray: Eternal God, you have come to
us in Jesus Christ, given us a new birth by water and the
Holy Spirit, and forgiven all our sins. Bless us now with the
grace we need to fulfill what we have promised.

PEOPLE: Keep us faithful to our Savior Jesus Christ,
for ever and ever. Amen.[4]

As the service of prayer concludes, the choir or congregation
sing a hymn, and leaders move among the congregation sprin-
kling the people with water from basins, using sprigs from a tree.
Following the affirmation of baptism, the eucharist is served.

The "Renewal of Baptismal Vows" is a service that has become very popular in the United Church of Christ. It is frequently

used at Conference Annual Meetings, National Board and Committee retreats, and in congregations. The liturgy is attractive because it is rich in symbolism and dramatically engages worshipers in remembering their baptism and keeping its power alive in their hearts and minds.

As with the service of confirmation, there is a provision for Holy Communion to be offered following the renewal of baptismal vows. It seems clear that these liturgies were crafted to encourage participants to understand the rites of Christian initiation as a holistic process rather than as separate rites and sacraments.

In keeping with these perspectives, we suggest that regular moments when the transforming presence of the Holy Spirit is confirmed can help Christians of all ages remember their baptism. We all need opportunities to say "yes" to those times when we have known God intimately. Such sharing strengthens our conviction that God cares for us and intercedes on our behalf. It also helps us grow in our ability to trust God to guide our lives. Repeatable rites of confirmation can offer the church a structure to focus on these faith-strengthening moments.

Once we have accepted the theological integrity of repeatable rites of confirmation, many important practical questions need to be answered.

- How do we envision repeatable rites of confirmation occurring in the life of the church?
- Who would participate?
- What are the critical moments in the lives of Christians during which this rite should be celebrated?
- What kinds of faith-strengthening opportunities need to be anticipated in order to envision confirmation as a life-long process?
- At what moments in the worship life of a congregation would a service of confirmation be included?

We can begin to answer all of these questions if we are clear that confirmation is designed to do three things. First, the rite of confirmation accompanies the sacrament of baptism and is the sign and seal of the presence of the Holy Spirit in the life of every baptized Christian. This initial confirmation is a time when the church says "yes" to the transforming effect of God's spirit in the lives of newly baptized Christians. Second, repeatable rites of confirmation are times when Christians of all ages are offered opportunities to say "yes" to their baptism by responding to moments when their faith has been strengthened. Third, repeatable rites of confirmation are the occasions when the entire body of believers can celebrate a strengthening of faith in the lives of its members.

A congregation might offer repeatable rites of confirmation at several significant stages during the spiritual journeys of its members. We have already suggested that each time there is a baptism, confirmation should be an integral part of the service. We suggest an appropriate act of confirmation would be the laying-on of hands and prayer following baptism in water. Those desiring an even more symbolic rite of confirmation can also offer a chrism during the laying-on of hands to seal the baptism. Finally, we have noted that Holy Communion should also be offered as a part of the unified rites of initiation. This can be performed by moistening the lips of the infant with a bit of bread and juice from the cup. When an older child, youth, or adult is baptized, the church says "yes" to a new member of the body of Christ in the same way. Adult initiation into the community of faith can be conducted in a very powerful way by adopting the process of the new Roman Catholic rites of initiation that require catechetical preparation for becoming a part of the body of Christ, followed by a unified rite of baptism, confirmation, and communion which initiates a believer into the faith community.[5]

Beyond the first rites of Christian initiation, we suggest that confirmation be repeated at those moments during a person's spiritual journey when faith has been strengthened. We believe that each age offers significant opportunities for growth in faith. Of course, individuals grow in faith in many different ways. Repeatable rites of confirmation need to be flexible, not dogmatic. We need to approach planning liturgy with an openness to God's unpredictable activity in human lives. At the same time, we believe that each age offers certain archetypal opportunities for strengthening faith. These opportunities are outlined in the following table:

*Children*

A strengthening of faith is confirmed as God images are acquired and Holy Communion is prepared for.

*Youth*

A strengthening of faith is confirmed as identity and relationships are experienced, faith is tested, and the decision to affirm one's place in the faith community is entertained.

*Younger Adult*

A strengthening of faith is confirmed as one's vocation is chosen and revealed.

*Adult*

A strengthening of faith is confirmed as one's lifestyle is crystallized with particular attention to the development of one's interior spiritual life.

*Elders*

A strengthening of faith is confirmed as one experiences life changes such as retirement and new beginnings, maturing faith and, eventually, death.

We believe that repeatable rites of confirmation can appropriately occur at each of these transitional moments. Children can confirm their faith as they develop a conscious relationship with God and prepare to receive Holy Communion in a more intentional way. Youth can confirm their faith as they test their beliefs, develop a Christian identity, explore the meaning of relationships, affirm their membership in the body of Christ, or choose to express their spiritual convictions in the world. Younger adults can confirm their faith as they consider the vocation to which God is calling them or explore how the spirit is shaping their witness in the world. Adults can confirm their faith as they seek to develop a Christian lifestyle or deepen their spiritual life.

Finally, elders can confirm their faith as they experience the deepest questions of meaning and the purpose of life.

These varied confirmable moments can each be prepared for through faith-forming education and celebrated through liturgy and ritual action. Christians need theological resources that help them discern the will of God at these different stages of their spiritual journeys. Members of each age and setting of life should benefit from confirmation curricula that encourage them to live out their baptism. For example, the teaching ministries needed for each of the five confirmable moments we have suggested can be summarized in the following way:

| Age | Confirmable Moments | Needed Teaching Ministries |
| --- | --- | --- |
| Children | Relational faith | Basic spiritual formation in acquiring of first God images in church school and home including preparation for communion. |
| Adolescents | Searching Faith: Identity, relationships, affirming church membership | Faith formation that gives permission to searching faith and builds lasting relationships in the church. |
| Younger Adults | Focusing Faith: Discovering one's vocation | Discerning God's call. |
| Adults | Manifesting Faith | How we live out our faith in community and the world |
| Elders | Surrendering and Separating Faith | Living with new beginnings, maturing faith |

What we are offering is a flexible, holistic approach to confirmation through which Christians can find diverse opportunities to say "yes" to faith-forming moments in their lives. Such an inclusive approach to confirmation has been resisted because the historic Reformed denominations have customarily limited confirmation to the teenage years. Some have suggested that this age-specific orientation is justified by the need for definitive Christian rites of passage into adulthood. This view attracts support because it provides a way to offer a desperately needed program of faith formation for youth and a socially acceptable rite of passage in a society that has no clear lines of demarcation between adolescence and adulthood.

There are many good reasons to offer ministries that help youth on the journey from childhood to adulthood. Adolescence is a time of enthusiastic dreaming and vision-seeking. Youth have a lively, seeking faith that leads them to experiment with intimacy in relationships, question their values and identity, and discover places where they fit in. The church needs to be a supportive community that instructs youth in the art of exploring life's possibilities in responsible ways. We need to challenge, encourage, and nurture their tentative spirituality. As we consider the stresses and challenges of growing up, it would be hard to offer too much spiritual guidance and encouragement to today's teenagers. A particularly useful exploration of a ministry that helps youth to journey from childhood to adulthood is *Initiation to Adulthood*, by William O. Roberts, Jr.[6] While we disagree that the program presented in this book represents an adequate model for confirmation, we commend it as a powerful and visionary ministry to youth.

Ministry with teenagers that provides rites of passage into adulthood is not synonymous with the rite of confirmation. Initiation into adulthood marks a physiological transition (puberty) and psychological transformation (individuation) in the lives of boys and girls that suggest it is time for them to assume adult roles in the tribe or society of which they are a part. Teenage confirmation does not particularly have to do with "coming of age." Rather, it is one time among many when Christians baptized into Christ's church have the opportunity to say "yes" to faith-strengthening moments in their lives. When we try to equate the educational process of teenage confirmation with rites of passage into adulthood, we once again confuse its purpose and cause it to lose its power.

When we examine the classical understanding of rites of passage, we find that they are more similar to the unified rites of Christian initiation than contemporary confirmation programs for youth. Victor Turner offers a helpful description of rites of passage into adulthood in his essay "Betwixt and Between: The Liminal Period in Rites of Initiation."[7] In this work, Turner suggests that rites of passage "reach their maximal expression in small-scale, relatively stable and cyclical societies, where change is bound up with biological and meteorological rhythms." These, of course, include such events as birth or puberty.

Arnold van Gennep provides further insights about rites of passage by defining three phases that characterize them:
1. *Separation* from one's previous reality
2. *Liminality,* during which one lives between one's old and new identity
3. *Aggregation,* during which one is integrated into a new identity and understanding of the world

In the Christian tradition, it is the unified rites of initiation— including baptism, first confirmation, and first communion—that conform to these traditional definitions of rites of passage. In the unified rites, we perceive an action bound up with biological and meteorological rhythms, as newborns are initiated into the body of Christ on holy days of the Christian year. Separation is experienced as initiates die to the world. Liminality occurs as they await their rebirth in Christ. Finally, aggregation is the result of being received into the body of Christ.

Youth confirmation programs represent none of these transitions. Rather, they provide an opportunity for adolescents to examine their lives and consider how faith can help them to find special meaning and purpose. If the historic Protestant churches wish to provide a definitive rite of passage into adulthood, it would mean normalizing catechesis and adult baptism and offering them in a unified rite (along with confirmation and Holy

Communion) to initiate youth into spiritual adulthood. As we have pointed out, to follow this path would be to adopt the baptismal theology of the radical reformers, who asserted that becoming Christian should be the consequence of intense preparation, committed belief, and a desire for conversion. The Roman Catholic document *Rite of Christian Initiation of Adults* offers a contemporary model for this approach which has much to commend it, especially the sort of ambitious challenge that can help adults or youth feel as if they are passing from their previous existence into a new identity in the body of Christ.

But the historic Protestant denominations are not prepared to limit themselves to believers' baptism. For us, baptism is not usually the consequence of intense preparation or the desire for conversion to Jesus Christ. It is more commonly the desire to receive the promise of God's saving grace. As the United Church of Christ *Book of Worship* observes:

> In the United Church of Christ people are baptized either as children or adults. Baptism with water and the Holy Spirit is the mark of their acceptance into the care of Christ's church, the sign and seal of their participation in God's forgiveness and the beginning of their new growth into full Christian life and faith.[8]

As long as we baptize infants and confirm the presence of the Holy Spirit in their lives through prayer and the laying-on of hands, we initiate new Christians into the church, not as a consequence of their "coming of age," but of the graciousness of God. While it is undeniably true that the church needs to do much more to provide decisive rites of passage into adulthood in its ministries and liturgies with youth, confirmation is not the appropriate vehicle to achieve this goal.

We noted earlier that, because of conventional wisdom about confirmation, many in the church feel it is necessary to limit confirmation to the teenage years. They suggest that its fundamental purpose is to offer youth the opportunity to become full members of the church. While such an opportunity is an important consequence of confirmation for youth, it is not the reason for confirmation.

Of course, we need to continue to offer youth a concentrated faith-formation education that culminates in the opportunity to affirm their baptism and remain members of the church. But this dimension of confirmation needs to be seen in the context of a more holistic process of faith formation that offers Christians of all ages and life situations the opportunity to confirm their faith and live out their baptism. In other words, we need repeatable rites of confirmation with youth faith formation playing a *valuable* role in the greater drama of becoming Christian.

A common objection to the proposal that confirmation be a repeatable rite is the assertion that repetition would cheapen the meaning of the rite. But to repeat a significant sacrament or rite of the church is not necessarily to devalue it. The sacrament of Holy Communion, for instance, is repeated regularly and serves as an irreplaceable symbol of nurture. In the same way, repeatable rites of confirmation can enliven our memories of our baptism and inspire us to be more aware of the ways that the Holy Spirit is guiding us into full Christian life and faith.

Others assert that it is theologically inappropriate to make confirmation a repeatable rite. How should we respond to this concern? In the first place, we acknowledge that the rites of the church must be carefully studied to ascertain and safeguard their historical integrity. It is not appropriate to alter the rites of the church merely to make them more relevant. It is clear, for instance, that baptism is a one-time, definitive, and decisive sacrament. It is equally clear that Holy Communion is expected to be a repeatable rite in which Christians participate often in remembrance of Christ. As we have seen, confirmation is a rite whose role is less clear than that of baptism or communion, but some critical theological insights have emerged in our exploration. Most crucial is the knowledge that confirmation can have no adequate theological meaning apart from baptism and Holy Communion. Aidan Kavanagh writes:

> It has often been forgotten that confirmation, so far from being a sovereign and self-contained sacrament, is held in being by two powerful and overlapping gravitational fields, so to speak. One is that exerted by baptism, the other by eucharist. Weaken either of

55

> *these two fields and confirmation flies out of orbit and is in danger*
> *of mutating into something alien to the tradition.*[9]

To keep confirmation in its traditional theological orbit, we have stressed that the rite must maintain its connection to baptism and eucharist in a unified rite of Christian initiation. But we also have argued that confirmation must offer baptized members of the community of faith ongoing opportunities to live out their baptism. There needs to be a process of confirmation through which Christians can confirm their faith at various times in their lives.

If we limit the rite of confirmation to any one moment in time and insist upon making it the only occasion on which Christians can affirm their baptism, we ignore the rich variety of ways the faith of Christians is strengthened.

To structure the rite of confirmation as a lifelong process of the living out of one's baptism, we not only need to identify the confirmable moments in Christian's lives, but we also need to provide a sequence of educational and liturgical experiences that help them to say "yes" to those times when their faith has been strengthened.

Maria Harris has suggested that a holistic sequence for Christian education should involve five biblical dimensions of learning:[10]

1. *Kerygma* or Proclamation
2. *Didache* or Teaching and Learning
3. *Leiturgia* or Worship and Prayer
4. *Koinonia* or Community Life with Others
5. *Diakonia* or Caring Service for Others[11]

A lifelong ministry of confirmation needs to incorporate these five elements, for they are essential ways of learning that equip us to live out our faith. Of course, they cannot be addressed adequately in one brief confirmation program for youth. If we wish to offer a ministry of spiritual formation that helps faith to mature throughout life, then we need educational models by which Christians can experience many different ways of strengthening their faith. A more broadly conceived process of confirmation would allow the church to reach out to persons of all ages with multiple opportunities to confirm their faith. By correlating the five dimensions of learning suggested by Maria Harris with the confirmable moments that persons encounter on their faith journey, a lifelong process of confirmation might look like this:

| Age | Confirmable Moment | Teaching Ministry Needed |
| --- | --- | --- |
| Children | Development of God images | Leiturgia—worship and prayer |
| Adolescents | Identity, relationships, values | Koinonia—community |
| Young Adults | God's call, vocation | Diakonia—serving Didache—learning |
| Adults | Lifestyle, spiritual formation | Didache—learning Diakonia—serving |
| Elders | Maturing faith, new beginnings, acceptance of death, sharing of wisdom | Kerygma—witnessing |

The table suggests that each confirmable moment in the lives of Christians can be addressed by a major teaching emphasis. Maria Harris suggests in her work that all five elements (*Kerygma, Didache, Leiturgia, Koinonia,* and *Diakonia*) are interrelated and need to be combined in an intergenerational process of education. Harris's book *Fashion Me a People* offers many helpful suggestions for integrating these educational understandings into the common life of congregations.

In our perspective of faith-forming education, the church would offer Christians at each stage of their spiritual journey the particular resources they need to live out their baptism. Of course, the particular experiences need to be contextual and age-appropriate. Children are more likely to strengthen their faith by learning to love God (*Leiturgia*) and by participating in a caring community (*Koinonia*) than by serving others or proclaiming the faith. Youth will generally respond most intensely to faith-forming education in community (*Koinonia*) and to the idealism of service (*Diakonia*). Adults will tend to experience confirmation as a time to reflect on the challenge of living out one's faith in the world (*Didache* and *Diakonia*). Confirmation for elders involves offering them the opportunity to teach and share stories of their faith (*Kerygma* and *Didache*).

We want to stress that faith formation strategies for repeatable rites of confirmation cannot be used rigidly. At times we will discover that unexpected issues and educational opportunities will arise. These need to be honored. We need to be flexible in planning faith-formation programs and repeatable rites of confirmation, so we don't create yet another stylized confirmation "program." Our desire is not to impose rigid guidelines on the rite of confirmation. Rather, we offer our vision as an elastic framework for acknowledging and celebrating the presence of the Holy Spirit in the lives of Christians.

Flexible faith-formation programs that address the essential faith-strengthening moments in the lives of Christians help us to have a well-rounded discipleship. We again want to encourage a process of continual faith formation punctuated by confirmation rites when Christians say "yes" to their baptism, and the church says "yes" to them.

We have repeatedly suggested that confirming such faith-strengthening moments could become the process through which the church nurtures its baptized members.

Many of the Psalms serve as excellent biblical illustrations of the ways in which people of faith can confirm their faith in many different life circumstances. A particularly powerful example is Psalm 107, which offers us a model of the ways the children of Israel experienced God's guidance:

> *O give thanks to God, for God is good;*
> *for God's steadfast love endures forever.*
> *Let the redeemed of God say so,*
> *whom God has redeemed from trouble*
> *and gathered in from the lands. . . .*

*Whoever is wise should give heed to these things;*
*let people consider the steadfast love of God.*[12]

Like the psalmist, we want to urge members of the community to "consider the steadfast love of the Lord" and praise God whenever faith is strengthened. We believe this especially appropriate on major holy days. For instance, following the initiation of new Christians on Easter Sunday, Pentecost, or Epiphany, members of the congregation could affirm their baptism, and all would then participate in a service of Holy Communion, beginning with the newly baptized. Following this special part of the eucharist, all baptized Christians would come forward to partake of the bread and cup. Other special services could also occur on Pentecost, Epiphany, All Souls' Day, or other special times during the church year. These services would recall God's great deeds in members' lives that have resulted in faith strengthening.

Repeatable rites of confirmation in our services of worship would unify the church's teaching ministry by ritualizing the key confirmable moments in the spiritual journeys of Christians. Young children who are acquiring their first images of God could benefit from a faith formation program in which they learn about the love of God and share biblical stories about the ways that people of faith throughout the centuries have experienced God's caring and compassion. This is also an excellent time in the life of the church to provide communion education, so that children can experience the ways Christ feeds them. The liturgy of the church can reinforce this educational experience by providing moments in the worship life of the church during which these young children are prayed for, that faithful God images might visit them.

Teenagers need opportunities to develop their identity as children of God and experience a community in which they can be accepted for who they are. Faith-forming education and liturgy can empower youth to know that, in the midst of their search for meaning and significance, they are accepted by God and supported by a family of faith. Where these teachings are experienced, many youth will naturally choose to affirm their church membership because they sense the Christian community is a place that accepts them and helps them to know who they are on a deeper level. The worship life of the church needs to give youth plenty of opportunities to praise God in the context of community.

Younger adults pursuing vocational hopes and dreams need practical spiritual disciplines through which they can seek God's empowerment in the charting of their future. Faith forming education for this group should provide knowledge of such disciplines. Liturgy can also play a significant role in the lives of younger adults. Before a young adult goes off to college or begins a new job, the entire congregation could join in worship to celebrate the vocational choices of their young people and pray God's rich blessing upon their search for meaning in their work. In turn, younger adults can confirm their faith by testifying to the ways that God is present in their lives.

Adults will respond to faith-forming educational opportunities which lead them to confirm their faith in relation to their lifestyles and primary relationships and through the enrichment of their spiritual lives. When they experience a strengthening of faith, the church can celebrate these moments in yet another liturgy of confirmation.

Elders need opportunities to confirm their faith in the midst of changes in life accompanying the beginnings of retirement, changing physical realities, and new extended family patterns.

It is easy to see that, when confirmation is applied to each of these age groups, we have an ongoing opportunity to discover the many ways that God gifts us with meaning, purpose, and grace.

Our model seeks to hold two central elements of education in tension. On the one hand, it provides the church with a structure to engage in practical theological reflection that connects daily living with the reality of God, thereby discovering how God is present. On the other hand, our model offers liturgical and scriptural images that set forth visions of the reign of God. When congregations provide meaningful educational opportunities for individuals to connect God to the actual experiences in their lives and supplement this pattern of personal theological reflection with the church's historic proclamation good things happen. We like the way Richard Osmer defines these two educational elements in his book *A Teachable Spirit*:

> The heart of practical theology is reflection that takes place in the midst of unfolding situations emerging out of social practices in an attempt to shape actional responses that are appropriate to what can be discerned of God's purposes for the world as they are brought to bear on the unique contexts of experience. . . . However, it is extremely important that images and concepts consistent with universalizing faith be kept alive in the preaching and teaching of the church. . . . Every time the church receives communion, it has the opportunity of bringing before it images of the messianic banquet in which persons from north and south, east and west will sit at the table of God. Every time portions of scripture are read that portray Jesus' proclamation of the kingdom of God, the church has the chance to hear of the universal reach of God's love and concern.[13]

At first glance, this holistic understanding of confirmation may seem overwhelming. One can almost hear overworked pastors and church educators groaning at the thought of offering a lifetime of faith-formation classes and experiences for every member. But if we reflect on the opportunity, we may find that an understanding of confirmation as a repeatable rite through which persons can prepare for and testify to God's presence in their lives can unify the church's teaching ministry.

We are proposing that confirmation can become the liturgical and educational umbrella for lifelong learning and growth on the Christian pilgrimage. In the next chapter, we will offer practical examples of faith-forming education for each confirmable moment in the life of a Christian. For now, the essential point to understand is that an intentional process of confirmation can unite the church's eclectic array of educational programs and ground them in the challenge of living out our baptism as members of the Body of Christ.

## DISCUSSION QUESTIONS

1. Share your reactions to the concept that confirmation can become the liturgical and educational umbrella for life-long learning and growth on the Christian pilgrimage.
2. Share moments in the church when you have enjoyed the opportunity to say "yes" to a strengthening of faith in your life.
3. How has the church most meaningfully affirmed a time of faith-strengthening in your life?
4. How would you most like your congregation to say "yes" to faith-strengthening moments in members' lives?
5. How might you encourage some of these new possibilities to happen in your church?

## CHAPTER FIVE

# Age-Appropriate, Faith-Forming Education for Living Out Our Baptism

In the previous chapter, we suggested that confirmation could occur at five critical moments of transition in the lives of Christians. These times are:

1. *Children*—the confirming of God images and preparation for Holy Communion
2. Youth—the confirming of one's identity as faith is tested in the midst of relationships and community; affirming one's baptism and membership in the church
3. Younger adults—the confirming of vocation and life exploration
4. Adults—the confirming of lifestyle, relationships, and one's personal spiritual life
5. Elders—the confirming of maturity, changing physical realities, new beginnings in retirement, new family realities, and accepting death

We now want to portray several educational models that can help persons in these various stages of life confirm their faith. We do not pretend that these critical moments of transition in the lives of Christians are the only times repeatable rites of confirmation should occur, nor do we suggest that every congregation should offer faith formation in a stylized way. As we have noted, repeatable rites of confirmation need to be flexible and contextual. To be effective, they must emerge from the actual faith journeys of members rather than be programmed. None-theless, we can expect that certain transitions in the lives of Christians are more common than others. We offer the follow-ing examples of repeatable rites of confirmation not as respon-sibilities every congregation must fulfill, but as "trail markers" that can help congregations plan for rites of confirmation that say "yes" to faith-strengthening moments throughout members' lives. We also suggest that wider settings of the church can do much to unify the teaching ministry by providing resources for teaching and learning that explore these various stages of life and encourage members of all ages to confirm their faith in new ways.

## CHILDREN, GOD IMAGES, AND HOLY COMMUNION

A powerful confirmable moment in childhood is the acquir-ing of the first God images. In her influential book *The Birth of the Living God*, Ana-Maria Rizzuto suggests that a child begins ac-quiring images of God about the age of five:

> *God is found in the family. Most of the time [God] is offered by the parents to the child; [God] is found in everyday conversation, art, architecture. [God] is presented as invisible but nonetheless real. Finally, most children are officially introduced to the "house of God," a place where God supposedly "dwells" one way or an-other. . . . The child is introduced to ritual, to the official behavior he is expected to exhibit there and to other events in which the en-counter with God is socially organized and prearranged. But the child brings his own God, the one he himself has put together, to this official encounter. Now, the God of religion and the God of the child-hero face each other. . . . This second birth of God may decide the conscious religious future of the child. This is the critical mo-ment for those interested in catechesis.*[1]

Rizzuto suggests that our first God images are worked out as our religious imagination is stimulated by the world in which we are socialized. Through an ongoing process of wondering, fan-tasizing, testing, reshaping, and rethinking, our personal representation of God gradually evolves. These first God images are critical, for they form the foundation of our spiritual identity.

The church can offer a special ministry of spiritual formation to children by guiding them to bond with healthy and faithful images of God. In the early stages of their faith, children need consistent opportunities to envision the God who is love. In a practical sense, this means providing educational, spiritual, and liturgical experiences for children to touch and be touched by the sacred.

Theological reflection offered during this early confirmable moment can be expressed through the wealth of biblical stories and images that proclaim God to be a loving, compassionate Creator who is present in our daily lives, sharing our joys and bearing our sorrows. This biblical theology should be offered by "telling the story" and creating moments for children to visualize the abiding presence of God who feeds the hungry with manna, frees the captives, heals those who are lame, and give us new life. During this early stage of faith strengthening, children can confirm their faith by "wondering," as Lois Rosko puts it, about the delicious mystery of God.

As scripture teases the spiritual imaginations of young children, it is valuable to help them portray God through song and visual art. This may include drawing pictures of the love of God that can be shared with parents and others in the congregation. It might involve planting flowers on the church grounds. It might include participation in the liturgy of the church, where children can light candles, sing a hymn, share their insights and feelings, or otherwise testify to God's love. Finally, confirming first God images should include the teaching of simple prayer techniques that encourage relationships with God. Children need to know that God is not remote or indifferent, but the parent of us all who can be trusted to care for us.

Children are also ready to learn many of the stories about Jesus. The life and ministry of Jesus provides an incarnational dimension of theological education. In Christ, children can reflect on the nature of God in a person and learn how God's values can be lived out in the human community.

A special word needs also to be said about Holy Communion and children. Many parents and children express a desire to participate regularly in the sacrament of Holy Communion. We believe this is a healthy impulse. Exposure to the transforming power of the eucharist is essential in the acquiring of first God images. As nothing else, Christ's simple meal exposes children to God's nurture and transforming love. The bread and cup are the essential way that the church says to its baptized members, "taste and see that God is good." For this reason, we have suggested that first communion for Christians should be included in unified rites of initiation. We now suggest that baptized children, as full members of the body of Christ, should continue to receive the bread and cup and, as they are ready, should learn about the mystery of the sacrament. In this way, children's faith will be strengthened as they come to see the church as a community where lives are transformed through the grace of God. This theological understanding is articulated clearly in the United Church of Christ *Book of Worship*:

> By baptism, a person becomes a member of Christ' s church and is
> welcome at Christ's table. For the newly baptized, the journey is
> from the font to the feast of the table.[2]

In addition to exposing little ones to God's love, childhood participation in the eucharist provides powerful experiences of Christian community. The passing of the bread and cup is a sign of the ways that brothers and sisters in Christ care for one another. Children who receive bread and the cup with the words of blessing learn far more about grace than those who are merely taught about belief.

We envision a curriculum in which children are initially offered opportunities to confirm their faith by experiencing the love of God in the Christian community. They would also be told stories by adult members of the congregation about the ways that Holy Communion has fed them, and they would be guided to be creatively present in worship. A confirmation curriculum for children might contain the following experiences:

1. Participating in bible stories, discussion, and creative visualization of the love of God, especially the life and teaching of Jesus Christ
2. Being presented with images and stories of the ways God feeds us with love
3. Learning simple prayer techniques that connect us with the love of God
4. Hearing stories from the elders of the ways they have experienced the love of God in bread and wine and been strengthened by it
5. Making bread for a eucharist service, and preparing the elements for the congregation
6. Continuing to participate in the eucharist and confirming first God images

## YOUTH, IDENTITY, AND COMMUNITY

Of all the age groups in the church, youth attract special concern. Perhaps this is the case because of their vulnerability. Youth stand upon a threshold between worlds. Parents often hold their breath, hoping that teenagers will not lose their way as they cross the boundaries between:

childhood and adulthood
dependency and autonomy
parental values and their own values
socialized identity and their own emerging identity
parental lifestyle and their own lifestyle
the familiar and the unknown
conformity and experimentation

Parents and adult friends of youth are always concerned that these transitions be approached in healthy ways. An important ministry to youth is to remind them that in the midst of their questioning, seeking, and exploring, they are still children of God. Faith-formation programs, leading to the rite of confirmation can help youth to know that they are valuable persons, with gifts to offer to the world.

Because of the intensity of the issues surrounding youth and their faith, the church must go to great lengths to provide a powerful faith-formation experience for them. A two-year program is not unreasonable, given the many ways youth need to grow in faith. We need not be afraid of creating faith-forming programs for youth which have strong content and offer intense experiences. Indeed, as currently practiced in most congregations, confirmation is already the major educational event for many Christians. It is one of the few times that parents will insist that their children attend an entire program of religious education aimed at a tangible goal. The church needs to make the most of this opportunity. We suggest that a substantive faith-formation experience for youth should contain five educational components:

1. Experiencing one's identity as a child of God
2. Strengthening one's identity as a part of the Christian community
3. Clarifying the meaning of healthy relationships
4. Enjoying the power and satisfaction of the Christian life
5. Participating in opportunities to serve and witness in the world

Each of these components needs to be considered in more detail.

Youth need a faith-formation program that helps them clarify their true identities. This focus should help them to discover both who they are and who they hope to be in light of the church's teaching that all persons are children of God. Depth psychology and traditional Christian spiritual disciplines need to be employed so that youth learn to discern their spiritual gifts, to love and trust themselves, to rely upon the love of God, and to seek their call in life.

Youth also need a faith-formation program that helps them experience the fact that they are not alone. Adolescence can be a time of weighty introspection and isolation. Experiences of disappointment, loss, and grief can reach a high level of emotional intensity. When teenagers are confronted with such questions as *Who am I?*, *Who values me?*, *Where am I going?*, or *What can I do with my life?*, it can seem as if one must bear the burden of these existential problems by oneself. Peer groups can help to meet the need for a supportive community in which teens can share their struggles and discoveries. Peer groups are important because they provide a place of acceptance and understanding, but such groups often lack the perspective adults can provide.

If youth explore their questions of identity only with peers, distortions can easily occur. In the worst cases, these distortions can lead to gang membership, drug abuse, cults, or cluster suicides. At the very least, such distortions can lead to indulgence in momentary experiences, moodiness, and withdrawal. The church can offer a significant ministry of faith formation by inviting youth to share their life journeys in a multigenerational community. In our fragmented society, it often seems as if youth have been exiled to peer penal colonies where they are expected to work out their identity in isolation from the adult world. The church is one of the very few places that can offer persons of different ages the opportunity to join together in the same activities. At its best, the Christian community can provide gatherings in which the peer friendships of youth can be supplemented by the counsel of supportive adults. Youth advisors, church educators, and pastors can become friends and companions with youth who are working out questions of identity. In the process, it becomes clear to youth that helpful adult guidance and encouragement can be found in the church. When youth know that they can share their concerns and have those concerns received with respect, they begin to discover that they are not alone after all, but cared for. It is then that personal change can occur on several levels. Youth who doubt their worth or creativity can find a way to express their spiritual gifts through adult encouragement. Those who are mourning a lost love or hope can find strength in the support of understanding adults. Those who are searching for a place to belong can come to the church and experience an empowering encounter with Christians of many ages.

Although all of these issues can be addressed through educational and liturgical programs in the weekly programming of the church, faith-formation education for youth should not be limited to congregation-based education. Identity, community, and relationship with God can also be discovered in places set apart—in retreat settings, at a church camp or on wilderness journeys, for example.

Congregations with the most vital faith-formation programs for youth characteristically offer retreat experiences in the wilderness or at church camps where youth can step aside from the distractions of their daily involvements, immerse themselves in new faith experiences, and peer more deeply into the majesty of life.

Many a campfire, lakeside worship, or wilderness sojourn has resulted in a decisive faith experience for youth. It is common for pastors to observe that church camping experiences were the places where they first experienced a call to ministry.

One youth group shared a week-long backpacking trip in the Colorado high country. On the sixth night, a severe storm pounded their camp. Several of the youth woke up with wet sleeping bags and clothing, anxious to hike out on the final day. The weather was uncertain and the route involved crossing a high, exposed pass. As they began to climb the pass, one young woman became increasingly nervous. When others asked her to explain her distress, she shared a vivid dream she'd had the previous night. In the dream, she had been alone on a mountain-top, crying, as lightning flashed over her head. The group took a break and decided to hold a dream council on the trail. Kathy told the group she was afraid that, if they continued to the summit, her dream would come true. The others in the group honored her feelings and tried to decide whether or not they should heed her intuitions. They searched the sky, but they saw no immediate danger of a storm. Although there were clouds, the weather seemed safe for travel, and the participants decided to go on. As the party neared the summit, dark clouds suddenly blew in and lightning erupted violently. The young people moved as quickly as they could across the summit and ran down the other side of the trail. The trip leaders feared what might happen if a member of the party were struck by lightning, but after several adrenalin-filled moments, everyone was safe. Below the pass, the youth took off their packs and sat upon boulders. Some cried, others sat

70

in thoughtful silence. For the next half hour, the youth shared stories of their intense awareness of their mortality and the prayers they had uttered to God in the midst of the storm. Faith was confirmed that day in a way that no written curriculum can offer.

Not all faith formation is a product of experience, however. A third dimension of confirmation has to do with catechesis, the formal process by which young Christians learn the content of faith. A responsible faith-formation program teaches what the church believes. Such teaching has to do with the life, ministry, death, and resurrection of Jesus Christ; with the mystery of God in the Hebrew Scriptures and the New Testament; and with the responsibilities of discipleship. Content is offered as a meaningful way to clarify and order faith. It helps young people to develop an adequate theology by reflecting on what they believe about the nature of God and God's will for their lives.

In the historic Protestant churches, many different styles of catechesis are offered. Some are quite formal, such as the Heidelberg Catechism, through which young persons are systematically instructed in the orthodox beliefs of the Reformed tradition. Others are more synthetic, such as the approach offered in the United Church of Christ resource, *Affirming Faith*. Here, we find a diverse faith-formation curriculum that includes not only the essential elements of belief within that denomination but also a good deal of reflection on such subjects as a Christian's relationship to her or his nation, personal identity, and the meaning of relationships. A strong catechetical component in a church's ministry of confirmation is essential, for it sets a tangible theological standard for mature, responsible faith. Without catechesis, it is all too easy to equate teenage confirmation with mere analysis of one's feelings or the subjective experiences of relationships and community. On the other hand, a faith-formation program that contains nothing but catechesis also inadequate because it fails to connect beliefs to the reality of teenage lives. What is most needed in our faith-formation curricula for youth is a holistic approach that breaks down the dichotomy between a conceptual catechesis on the one hand and experiential programs of education on the other. Today's youth need both of these approaches if they are to be inspired to be active members of the Christian community.

The fifth dimension of faith-formation education for youth is that of mission and servanthood. Youth learn by involvement, not just by the transmission of ideas. We need to do far more to create opportunities for our youth to become disciples in the world. Building a home with Habitat for Humanity, working in a homeless shelter, or performing other good works—all of these help youth understand the truth of Christ's teaching: "As you do unto the least of these, you do unto me." Mission and servanthood opportunities sensitize youth to the ways that caring can make a difference in the world. Mission often involves cross-cultural experiences that break down the stereotypes that separate rich from poor and one ethnic tradition from another. We suggest that every faith-formation program should contain work camps through which youth may serve.

It is valuable to offer youth the opportunity to affirm their membership in the church as a part of their confirmation experience. We have repeatedly stated that the decision to join the church is not the *reason* for offering confirmation to youth, for Christians become members of the church through baptism. Rather, choosing to belong to a congregation is an opportunity to respond to a caring community that has helped to strengthen one's faith in essential ways.

## YOUNGER ADULTS

Younger adults need an opportunity to confirm their vocation. The word *vocation* comes from the Latin word *vocare*, which means "to call." Mature Christian faith is based upon the recognition that God guides us to use our spiritual gifts on behalf of others and creation. As baptized Christians who are members of the body of Christ, we cannot find true satisfaction in our life until we are aware of God's purpose for us and express that purpose through our daily work.

Younger adults are filled with hopes and dreams for the future. This is a time of life when men and women explore what it means to make a difference in the world. It is also a time when they seek fulfillment by searching for a way to do that which they most love. Younger adults need guidance and counsel in order to discern their life's work and encouragement to persist in achieving the vocational dream to which God is calling them. Often, this quest involves balancing one's ideal with the demands of the real world. Perhaps you know a younger adult such as Mary, who wants very much to be an artist. She likes the challenge of capturing images that communicate the meaning of life in creative ways. After graduation from high school, she plans to go to photography school and then set up her own shop.

Mary could benefit from a faith-formation program that would help her discern her vocation more clearly. She knows she has a love for art, but she has not yet thought through the things she needs to do to express that love in a way that will both earn her a living and serve the world. Perhaps Mary will be one of the lucky few with sufficient talent to earn her way as an independent artist. But perhaps God is calling her to use her artistic gifts through another vocation such as teaching or ministry. To harmonize one's skills with God's desires and the realities of the world is a difficult challenge which faith-forming education can help to clarify. Faith-forming education for young adults needs not only to teach concepts but also to call forth the gifts of Christians. Young adults such as Mary can benefit from a faith-forming program that provides a place to share their artistic creativity. Many people never experience satisfaction in their jobs because no one has helped them express their talents or think beyond working for money. If we work only to achieve personal goals such as wealth, status, or power, satisfaction with our work remains incomplete. A sense of deeper meaning comes when we experience the ways our work can serve others or make a difference in the world. True joy comes when empowering others begins to delight us as much as fulfilling our own needs. The church can help its young adults to strengthen their faith by discerning how God wants them to improve the quality of life.

Celebrating the authentic vocational choices of younger adults is as important as helping them to clarify their vocation.

We need liturgies that bless those who are going forth to claim a vocation. Members who secure a job or are accepted to a university can have their faith strengthened by a congregation that confirms their choices.

Faith formation for younger adults can also involve helping parents to let go. Younger adults who graduate from high school often journey into spiritual exile. Robert T. Gribbon of the Alban Institute has characterized this time as a period of "suspension of belief" during which one explores and tests many faith options before committing oneself to a particular path.[3] Confirmation needs actively to encourage this period of suspension of belief by commissioning young adults to undertake their spiritual search while also calling upon God to guide their quest. Younger adults can be encouraged by the stories of older members of the church who share their own search for meaning. The church can stand ready to welcome younger adults whenever they return, and encourage them to share the knowledge they gained on their journeys.

## ADULTS: LIFESTYLE AND SPIRITUAL FORMATION

If youth and younger adults seek meaning in their lives, adults yearn for significance. Adults have already made vocational choices and committed themselves to particular lifestyles. Satisfaction during this period of life comes from knowing that one's choices are authentic. Just as younger adults need a vision that promises to make a difference in their lives, adults need confirmation that their lives make a difference for others.

In the Christian tradition, having a life that makes a difference is a matter of commitment to core spiritual values. This often involves the quest for a lifestyle that encourages peace and justice. The church can help its adult members to confirm their faith by offering models of ways of life that encourage Christian values. Mothers and fathers can confirm the values of Christian parenting. Single adults can confirm the values of friendship. All adults can confirm the values of stewardship. Regardless of the values being pursued, adults need opportunities to confirm their faith in the midst of their day-to-day lives. The more adult Christians become aware of faith's place in daily living, the more faith is strengthened.

We have suggested that much of the disillusionment of adult life is due to the lack of a vision greater than the pursuit of personal fulfillment. Adult faith formation can give persons a broader purpose for living. As adults seek a comfortable material existence, they need to move beyond possessing things to being possessed by eternal values.

The church can provide an important ministry of confirmation to adults who are seeking a system of spiritual meaning. We envision faith-forming education that helps adults identify the core values of Christian faith and provides opportunities to ground their lives in those values. In many cases, this will involve experiments in new lifestyles that give expression to gospel values. Adults need continually to be challenged to match the idealism of the gospel with the real things they can do in their lives. Few will choose to give themselves as a "sacrifice for many" in a literal sense, but most Christians do want to serve those who need help. Our members can strengthen their faith both by learning to care for others and by accepting the limits of their compassion. God offers many opportunities to heal but there are always more hurts than healers in our world. To love as Christ does, we must learn how to serve with joy yet also have the courage to accept that we cannot save the world through our own actions. Christian disciplines such as prayer, bible study, spiritual reading, and journaling can help adult Christians pursue the will of God for their lives and meet the challenges it offers. As adults discover deeper ways to live their faith, the congregation can confirm those moments of strengthening through the rite of confirmation.

## ELDERS: NEW BEGINNINGS, RETIREMENT, AND DEATH

Elders need a ministry of confirmation, too. Being an elder is a powerful position often trivialized by our society. In traditional cultures, elders possess the deepest experience and wisdom.

Their opinions are sought on all matters of consequence because they have learned much about the rhythms and seasons of life. The Christian church needs to do far more to honor the wisdom of its elders. We can do more by offering them opportunities to witness to what they have learned about the nature of God in the living of their lives. Elders have many stories and experiences to share that can give youth a deeper perspective about such things as birth and death, hope and suffering, joy, and grief. Elders can be commissioned to teach, and this commissioning is a wonderful way to confirm their faith and their values in the congregation.

Because many elders are retiring from jobs they held for many years, they also need opportunities to confirm their faith in the midst of a changing identity. On the one hand, this means letting go of old attachments and systems of meaning built upon one's working life. On the other hand, it means awakening to new opportunities to use one's talents and gifts. Retirement can be both exciting and frightening, depending upon one's life situation. The church needs to offer elders opportunities to retire with hope and faith. This not only means providing elders with opportunities to share their wisdom and experience within the congregation as mentors and teachers; it also means providing opportunities for them to seek God's guidance and blessing in the midst of this powerful life transition. Pre-retirement seminars, support groups, and educational classes that explore the dynamics of retirement and elderhood are just a few of the significant ways we can help our elders make their peace with retirement.

Also important are faith-forming experiences that help elders confirm faith in the face of changing realities of health, family, and death. The elder years are a time when the church's promise of resurrection assumes increasing significance. As we grow closer to the end of our lives, we all can benefit from opportunities to explore what our faith promises regarding salvation. Confirming one's faith on this level might include biblical and theological study about the Christian understanding of death, resurrection, and salvation; group reflections on the art of

76

letting go of this life; prayer groups; or the opportunity to leave a heritage for one's descendants. The church might confirm the faith of its elders through special memorial services for those who have died during the preceding year. All Saints' Day is a powerful time during the Christian year to celebrate the witnesses of those who have gone before as well as to honor the contributions of living elders in the community.

Regardless of our "age and stage" of life, confirmation awakens us to the Holy Spirit dwelling within us. It is the process by which we are reminded that God is our companion and friend. God's presence has often been described by Christian mystics as an inner fire that warms and illumines the darkness of the human heart. Two central biblical themes of God's nature are those of light and fire: God's light illuminates our path and keeps us from losing our way; God's fire creates a burning desire within us to offer hope to those who dwell in conditions of despair. Borrowing from the writings of Alan Jones, we suggest that the church must learn to confirm by "handing on fire":

> What are we going to hand on to the next generation? What do we hand on to our children? Do we hand on a life without a commitment? Do we hand on a life which is not marked by the keeping of promises? Do we hand on a life of lost integrity? Or do we hand on a life pregnant with promise because it is God's? Do we hand on a life full of hope because the future is God's? Do we hand on fire? There is a great deal at stake in our understanding ourselves as men and women of tradition in this lively sense. We are those who are called to hand on life. Fire is very dangerous. The flame of God's love will burn us before it will transform us. Our God is a consuming fire. We will be turned up either by the fire of God's love or the fire of our self-centeredness. Which will it be?[4]

A faithful process of confirmation reminds all members of the church that the fire of the Holy Spirit dwells within us as a gift of our baptism. A lifetime is required to confirm the effect God's fire has upon our lives. The spiritual imagination that is first kindled during childhood needs to be stoked by guides, mentors, and educators. The "burning questions" of identity, relationship, and vocation that occupy the lives of youth and younger adults require a caring community to bank the fire and keep it from going out. The quest of adults to forge a faithful lifestyle that witnesses to God's will in the world needs a community that will help them set a large log upon the fire and keep it burning. Elders need a community that will help them create a rich bed of coals that will glow in the valley of the shadow of death.

A faithful process of confirmation helps us to understand that being reborn through the Holy Spirit at the time of our baptism does not make our lives simpler, more predictable, or more secure. Rather, our baptism causes us to live differently than if we had no faith. We live differently because of the presence of divine possibility that will not give us peace until we find true rest in God. God's indwelling presence initiates us into a life of seeking and questioning. God's holy spirit encourages us to discover meaning beneath the surface of life and will not allow us to remain content with superficial answers. Thus, baptism sows the seeds of faithful discontent within the lives of everyone who is born of water and the word.

Of course, we believe that the discontent caused by baptism is ultimately made joyful by the blessings of God. When we become Christian, we are challenged yet not broken, tested but not overwhelmed. In this way, our faith is made mature.

Because baptism has this effect on every Christian, it is important for the church to offer to each member opportunities to reflect on the cost of their initiation into the body of Christ. Perhaps we adult Christians are too quick to anoint our children with water and too slow to help them to struggle with the implication of their rebirth in Christ. We need to provide Christians of all ages with resources to confront the cost of their baptism and awaken the transforming power of God in all the seasons of their lives.

Confirmation is both the process of learning new things and believing the "old, old story" of God's love. The Holy Spirit of God, said Jesus, is like a divine wind: "It blows where it will and no one know from whence it comes or where it goes" (John 3:8). This wind of the Spirit blows across the water in the baptismal font and causes each Christian to be reborn: "Truly, truly, I say to you, unless one is born of water and the Spirit he cannot enter the kingdom of God" (John 3:5). Yet, the winds of the Holy Spirit continue to direct us. Confirmation is the ongoing opportunity to surrender to the presence of the Spirit in our lives. In *The Way of the White Clouds*, Lama Govinda offers a poignant illustration of this act of surrender:

> *Just as a white summer cloud, in harmony with heaven and earth, freely floats in the blue sky from horizon to horizon following the breath of the atmosphere—in the same way the pilgrim abandons [oneself] to the breath of the greater life that . . . leads [one] beyond the farthest horizons to an aim which is already present within [one] although hidden from [one's] sight.[5]*

In order for faith to be strengthened, we need to say "Yes" to God's Holy Spirit, whether it is revealed to us as the greater breath of the atmosphere, as earthquake, as wind, as fire—or as a still, small voice that whispers to us in the night. We also need a community of friends in faith who honor one another's encounters with God and support one another's quests to respond adequately to God's call.

When Samuel was a boy sleeping in the Temple with his spiritual teacher Eli, the Holy Spirit of God came upon him and repeatedly whispered to him, "Samuel!" Hearing his name called, Samuel assumed that his teacher Eli was calling him. Two times, Samuel arose and went to Eli. But the priest said, "I did not call you, go back to sleep." The third time Samuel came, Eli discerned that the voice of God was at work. He counseled Samuel to return to his bed and confirm God's presence by dialoguing with the voice when it next was heard. Thus, when Samuel again heard the voice of God, he responded: "Speak, Lord, for thy servant listens" (1 Sam. 3:1–18). In turn, God called Samuel in a special way. The text reads: "Samuel grew up and YAHWEH was with him and let no word of his fall to the ground. All Israel . . . came to know that Samuel was accredited as a prophet" (1 Sam. 3:19–20).

Among other things, this is a story of the way confirmation

works in the lives of faithful people. For initiates such as the boy Samuel, who "do not yet know the Lord" (1 Sam. 3:7), confirmation is a process of awakening to a lifelong relationship with God. For elders such as Eli, confirmation is the process of helping others in the community discern God's presence in one's call. For the wider community of faith, confirmation is the process of saying "yes" to those who, like Samuel, begin a spiritual journey.

In his work *Acquiring Our Image of God*, Martin Lang suggests that one's faith is an overarching "life meaning system" that provides "an internal orienting of all other . . . systems."[6] A life meaning system is not merely an intellectual understanding of one's world. Rather, it is a complete faith orientation that encompasses the physical, emotional, and intellectual components of one's life. A life meaning system is born of an encounter between each person and his or her world. Lang suggests that six experiences lead to life meaning systems and give them life-directing power and influence:

1. Life meaning systems are built upon "impressive" and "landmark" experiences which possess deep emotional and symbolic force in one's life.
2. A powerful life meaning system is built upon a religious story offered by a faith community that corresponds with one's life experience. Life meaning systems are woven together from the warp of one's personal life experience and the woof of the communal story as one either inherits it or comes to know it.
3. A powerful life meaning system is grounded in a community in which persons can invest their creative gifts and practice a new way of life.
4. A life meaning system is enhanced by the ability of the community to convey new meaning and experiences of the nature of God.
5. A life meaning system is fueled by the visible presence of prayer.
6. A life meaning system generates its own convictional power by offering new ways to experience purpose in life.[7]

Life meaning systems are the product of faith-formation education which we envision as the lifelong process of confirmation. As Lang points out, constructing a life meaning system includes both catechetical study and faith-forming experiences which invite Christians to weave their own spiritual journeys into the biblical story. The rite of confirmation needs a "proclaiming curriculum," which helps confirmands to know the biblical story, practice the life of prayer, and care for others. Such a holistic view of confirmation can help persons of all ages to strengthen faith.

If we orient ourselves to the broader theological horizon, we will discover that confirmation can provide an overarching framework for the teaching ministry. Understood as an ongoing liturgical and educational process, confirmation can help us experience that—as John Chrysostom told the neophytes of the fourth century—"God's blessings and spiritual gifts abound on every side."

The rite of confirmation can regain its place in the church if it is understood as marking moments of faith-strengthening along the path of discipleship. As we practice confirmation as a process by which Christians say "yes" to their baptism, believers will be united with Christ. Augustine suggested that, when we are baptized, "the Holy Spirit dwells without our knowledge, in our being." Through a lifelong process of confirmation, we can progressively become aware of the divine image dwelling within us until Christ dwells in our hearts through faith and gives us, as Paul says,

> power to comprehend with all the Saints what is the breadth and
> length and height and depth, and to know the love of Christ which
> surpasses knowledge, that you may be filled with all fullness of
> God. (Eph. 3:16–19)

Paul's words provide us with a suitable confirmation prayer for our own age. It is our hope that God will lead us all through faith to use the historic rite of confirmation to deepen the dwelling of God in our hearts and root us in love.

## DISCUSSION QUESTION

A facilitator or leader of the group can invite participants to consider how their faith was strengthened at different stages of their spiritual journey:

*As a child*:
- How were your God images formed?
- Did you prepare for Holy Communion?

*As a youth*:
- How did you test the Christian faith in the midst of relationships and community?
- Did you affirm your membership in the church at that time?

*As a younger adult:*
- How did you discover your vocation?
- Did your church help?

*As an older adult*:
- How might confirmation help you to clarify your life?
- Did the church help you to deepen your spiritual life?

*As an elder*:
- Has the church helped you to confirm your faith in relation to retirement and death?

# Notes

## INTRODUCTION

1. Robert N. Bellah et al., *Habits of the Heart: Individualism and Commitment in American Life* (New York: Harper and Row, 1985), 84.

2. Henri Nouwen, *Reaching Out* (New York: Doubleday, 1975), 51.

## CHAPTER 1

1. Karl Rahner, *A New Baptism in the Spirit: Confirmation Today* (Renville, N.J.: Dimension Books, 1975), 5.

2. Loren B. Mead, *The Once and Future Church: Reinventing the Congregation for a New Mission Frontier* (Washington, D.C.: The Alban Institute, 1991), 28–29.

## CHAPTER 2

1. Michael Dujarier, "A Survey of the History of the Catechumenate," *Confirmation Re-examined*, ed. Kendig Cully (Wilton, Conn.: Morehouse-Barlow Co., 1982), 28.

2. Aidan Kavanagh, *Confirmation: Origins and Reform* (New York: Pueblo Publishing Co., 1988), 6.

3. H. Bettenson, *Documents of the Christian Church* (London: Oxford University Press, 1967), 64.

4. E. Yarnold, *The Awe Inspiring Rites of Initiation: Baptismal Homilies of the Fourth Century* (St. Paul, Minn.: Slough, 1972).

5. Yarnold, quoting St. Cyril of Jerusalem, *Awe Inspiring Rites*, 76–77.

6. Kavanaugh, *Confirmation*, 51.

7. Max Thurian, *Consecration of the Layman* (Baltimore: Helicon, 1963), 30–33.

8. Yarnold, quoting St. Cyril of Jerusalem, *Awe Inspiring Rites*, 80–81.

9. Mark Searle, *Christening: The Making of Christians* (Collegeville, Minn.: Liturgical Press, 1980), 119.

10. James White, *Sacraments as God's Self-Giving* (Nashville, Tenn.: Abingdon, 1983), 50.

11. Searle, *Christening*, 119.

12. Bishop Faustus of Riez, quoted in Searle, *Christening*, 118.

13. Council of Trent, II, iii, 17, translated by Donovan, 1829, 184.

14. Martin Luther, "The Babylonian Captivity of the Church," *Luther's Works*, vol. 36, Word and Sacrament II (Philadelphia: Muhlenberg Press, 1959), 92.

15. Ibid., 58–59.

16. Ibid. 68.

17. Ibid. 60–61.

18. Roland Bainton, *Christendom: A Short History of Christianity and Its Impact on Western Civilization* (New York: Harper, 1964), 38–39. Parenthetical statement added.

19. Ibid., 40.

# CHAPTER 3

1. *Book of Worship* (New York: UCC Office for Church Life and Leadership, 1986), 143.

2. John Westerhoff, *Will Our Children Have Faith: Bringing Up Children in the Christian Faith* (Minneapolis: Winston Press, 1980), 49.

3. *The Westminster Dictionary of Worship*, edited by J. G. Davies (Philadelphia: Westminster Press, 1979), 335.

4. Ibid., 336.

5. *Rite of Christian Initiation of Adults*, International Commission on English in the Liturgy (Collegeville, Minn.: The Liturgical Press, 1988), XVI.

6. Alexander Schmemann, *Liturgy and Life: Christian Development Through Liturgical Experience* (New York: Department of Religious Education, Orthodox Church in America, 1974), 97.

7. E. C. Whitaker, *Documents of the Baptismal Liturgy* (London, England: SPCK, 1970), 104.

8. Mark Searle, *Christening: The Making of Christians* (Collegeville, Minn.: The Liturgical Press, 1980), 153.

9. James White, *Sacraments as God's Self-Giving* (Nashville, Tenn.: Abingdon Press, 1983), 66.

10. Ibid., 66–67.

11. Tom Driver, *The Magic of Ritual: Our Need for Liberating Rites That Transform Our Lives and Our Communities* (San Francisco: Harper, 1991), 222.

12. Searle, *Christening*, 100.

## CHAPTER 4

1. *Book of Worship* (New York: UCC Office for Church Life and Leadership, 1986), 129.

2. Ibid., 145.

3. Ibid., 143.

4. Ibid., 240–41.

5. *Rite of Christian Initiation of Adults*, International Commission on English in the Liturgy (Collegeville, Minn.: The Liturgical Press, 1988). Roman Catholic colleagues in your area will probably be more than happy to share their experience with this rite.

6. Victor Turner, "Betwixt and Between: The Liminal Period in Rites of Passage," in *Betwixt and Between: Patterns of Masculine and Feminine Initiation*, ed. Louise Carus Mahdi, Steven Foster, and Meredith Little (La Salle, Ill.: Open Court, 1987), 4–5.

7. *Book of Worship*, 129.

8. Aidan Kavanaugh, *Confirmation: Origins and Reform* (New York: Pueblo Publishing, 1988), 88.

9. This schema is developed by Maria Harris in *Fashion Me a People: Curriculum in the Church* (San Francisco: Harper and Row, 1988).

10. *Inclusive Language Psalms* (New York: The Pilgrim Press, 1987).

11. Richard Robert Osmer, *A Teachable Spirit: Recovering the Teaching Office of the Church* (Louisville: Westminster/John Knox Press, 1990), 162, 215.

## CHAPTER 5

1. Ana-Maria Rizzuto, *The Birth of the Living God: A Psychoanalytic Study* (Chicago: University of Chicago Press, 1979), 8.

2. *Book of Worship*, 131.

3. See Robert T. Gribbon, "The Problem of Faith Development in Young Adults" (Washington, D.C.: The Alban Institute, 1977).

4. Alan Jones, *Exploring Spiritual Direction: An Essay on Christian Friendship* (New York: Harper and Row, 1982), 124.

5. In Peter Matthiessen, *The Snow Leopard* (New York: Bantam Books, 1979), 9.

6. Martin A. Lang, *Acquiring Our Image of God: Emotional Basis for Religious Education* (New York: Paulist Press, 1983), 25.

7. Ibid., 39.

# Bibliography

Bainton, Roland. *Christendom: A Short History of Christianity and Its Impact on Western Civilization*. New York: Harper, 1964. Parenthetical statement added.

Bellah, Robert N., et al. *Habits of the Heart: Individualism and Commitment in American Life*. New York: Harper and Row, 1985.

Bettenson, H. *Documents of the Christian Church*. London: Oxford University Press, 1967.

*Book of Worship*. New York: UCC Office for Church Life and Leadership, 1986.

Driver, Tom. *The Magic of Ritual: Our Need for Liberating Rites That Transform Our Lives and Our Communities*. San Francisco: Harper, 1991.

Dujarier, Michael. "A Survey of the History of the Catechumenate." In *Confirmation Re-examined*, ed. Kendig Cully. Wilton, Conn.: Morehouse-Barlow Co., 1982.

Gribbon, Robert T. "The Problem of Faith Development in Young Adults." Washington, D.C.: The Alban Institute, 1977.

Harris, Maria. *Fashion Me a People: Curriculum in the Church*. San Francisco: Harper and Row, 1988.

Jones, Alan. *Exploring Spiritual Direction: An Essay on Christian Friendship*. New York: Harper and Row, 1982.

Kavanagh, Aidan. *Confirmation: Origins and Reform*. New York: Pueblo Publishing Co., 1988.

Lang, Martin A. *Acquiring Our Image of God: Emotional Basis for Religious Education*. New York: Paulist Press, 1983.

Matthiessen, Peter. *The Snow Leopard*. New York: Bantam Books, 1979.

Mead, Loren B. *The Once and Future Church: Reinventing the Congregation for a New Mission Frontier*. Washington, D.C.: The Alban Institute, 1991.

Myers, William. *Becoming and Belonging: A Practical Design for Confirmation*. Cleveland: United Church Press, 1993.

Nouwen, Henri. *Reaching Out.* New York: Doubleday, 1975.

Osmer, Richard Robert. *A Teachable Spirit: Recovering the Teaching Office of the Church.* Louisville: Westminster / John Knox Press, 1990.

Ostermiller, R. Kenneth, ed. *Affirming Faith: A Congregation's Guide to Confirmation.* Cleveland: United Church Press, 1995.

Rahner, Karl. *A New Baptism in the Spirit: Confirmation Today* Renville, N.J.: Dimension Books, 1975.

*Rite of Christian Initiation of Adults,* International Commission on English in the Liturgy. Collegeville, Minn.: The Liturgical Press, 1988.

Rizzuto, Ana-Maria. *The Birth of the Living God: A Psychoanalytic Study.* Chicago: University of Chicago Press, 1979.

Schmemann, Alexander. *Liturgy and Life: Christian Development Through Liturgical Experience.* New York: Department of Religious Education, Orthodox Church in America, 1974.

Searle, Mark. *Christening: The Making of Christians.* Collegeville, Minn.: Liturgical Press, 1980.

*The Westminster Dictionary of Worship.* Edited by J. G. Davies. Philadelphia: Westminster Press, 1979.

Thurian, Max. *Consecration of the Layman.* Baltimore: Helicon, 1963.

Turner, Victor. "Betwixt and Between: The Liminal Period in Rites of Passage." In *Betwixt and Between: Patterns of Masculine and Feminine Initiation,* ed. Louise Carus Mahdi, Steven Foster, and Meredith Little. La Salle, Ill.: Open Court, 1987.

Westerhoff, John. *Will Our Children Have Faith: Bringing Up Children in the Christian Faith.* Minneapolis: Winston Press, 1980.

Whitaker, E. C. *Documents of the Baptismal Liturgy.* London: SPCK, 1970.

White, James. *Sacraments as God's Self-Giving.* Nashville: Abingdon, 1983.

Yarnold, E. *The Awe Inspiring Rites of Initiation: Baptismal Homilies of the Fourth Century.* St. Paul, Minn.: Slough, 1972.

# Index

89